100% NEW

DEVELOPING LITERACY

Photocopiable teaching resources f

Edge Hill University
WITHDRAWN

UNDERSTANDING AND RESPONDING TO TEXTS

Ages 6–7

Christine Moorcroft

A & C Black • London

Edge Hill University
Learning Services x

Barcode   799909

Published 2008 by A & C Black Publishers Limited
38 Soho Square, London W1D 3HB
www.acblack.com

ISBN 978-0-7136-8461-2

Copyright text © Christine Moorcroft 2008
Copyright illustrations © Moreno Chiacchiera/Beehive Illustration 2008
Copyright cover illustration © Piers Baker 2008
Editor: Jane Klima
Designed by Susan McIntyre

The authors and publishers would like to thank Ray Barker and Rifat Siddiqui for
their advice in producing this series of books.

The authors and publishers are grateful for permission to reproduce the following:

p.52: 'Sea Song' by James Kirkup, from *A Very First Poetry Book* (OUP).
Reproduced by permission of the author. p55: 'Bouncing' by Simon James, from
Days Like This: A Collection of Small Poems, edited by Simon James
(Candlewick). Reproduced by permission of Walker Books Ltd., London. Every
effort has been made to trace copyright holders and to obtain their permission for use of
copyright material. The authors and publishers would be pleased to rectify any error or
omission in future editions.

A CIP catalogue record for this book is available from the
British Library.

All rights reserved. This book may be photocopied for use in the school or
educational establishment for which it was purchased, but may not be
reproduced in any other form or by any means – graphic, electronic or
mechanical, including recording, taping or information retrieval systems – without
the prior permission in writing of the publishers.

Printed by Halstan Printing Group, Amersham, Buckinghamshire.

A & C Black uses paper produced with elemental chlorine-free pulp, harvested
from managed sustainable forests.

Contents

Introduction   5

Notes on the activities   6

Using the CD-ROM   12

Fiction

Stories in familiar settings

Sad to say   draw together ideas and information from across a whole text, using simple
                               signposts in the text   13

Granny's Jungle Garden   identify characters and describe them   14

Amazing Grace   identify the feelings, personality and talents of the main character   15

Leon and Bob story map   identify the main events of a story and retell them in the correct order   16

Feelings   explore how particular words are used, including words and
                               expressions with similar meanings   17

Traditional stories

Character match   identify characters from descriptions of them   18

What if...?   draw together ideas and information from across a whole text   19

Faces   explain how illustrations affect a reader   20

That's not right   explain organisational features of a text and identify what illustrations show about a story   21

Let's ask Rapunzel   engage with books through exploring and enacting interpretations   22

Different stories by the same author

Character quest   draw together ideas and information from across a whole text, and give reasons why
                               characters change   23

Book log   read whole books on their own   24

About the author   investigate a particular author   25

Extended stories by significant children's authors

Story tracker   understand the structure of a longer story   26

Reasons   give some reasons why things happen   27

Cliffhanger   predict what might happen next   28

Character clues   explore how particular words are used   29

The story judge   explain their reactions to texts, commenting on important aspects   30

Non-fiction

Instructions

Hide and seek   read and follow instructions   31

Ladybird program   read and follow precise instructions   32

Stripy lolly   explain and follow organisational features of texts, including layout, diagrams,
                               captions and numbering   33

Simon says   use understanding of syntax and context to differentiate between descriptions
                               and instructions   34

Explanations

Dragon life cycle   explain and use organisational features of texts, including layout, diagrams, captions
                               and bullet points   35

Fairyland   explain and use organisational features of texts, including layout and bullet points   36

Buildings glossary: 1	explain organisational features of a text, including alphabetical order, layout, diagrams and captions	37
Buildings glossary: 2	explain organisational features of a text, including alphabetical order, layout, diagrams and captions	38

Information texts

Miss Muffet's friends	explain organisational features of a text, including alphabetical order and layout	39
Fairytale facts	explain organisational features of a text, including alphabetical order and layout	40
Look it up	use the alphabetically ordered text of a dictionary to find information	41
Book skimmer	choose a book and justify selection	42
Web skimmer	choose a website and justify selection	43
Answer finder	scan a text in order to locate specific information	44
Seashore scanner	scan a text in order to locate specific information	45

Non-chronological reports

Island reports	explain organisational features of a text, including alphabetical order, layout, diagrams, captions, hyperlinks and bullet points	46
Island fact-file	use a website in order to find specific information	47
Key words map	record information from non-fiction books and websites	48
Guy Fawkes information race: 1	use websites and information books in order to find specific information	49
Guy Fawkes information race: 2	explain organisational features of a text, including alphabetical order, layout, diagrams, captions, hyperlinks and bullet points	50
Note it	explain organisational features of a text, including layout and a key	51

Poetry

Patterns on the page

Sea song	explore and predict rhyming patterns and repeated language	52
Anna Elise	engage with a text through exploring and enacting interpretations	53
Fire! Fire!	complete rhyming sentences	54
Bouncing	engage with a text through exploring and enacting interpretations	55
Shape match	explain and use organisational features of texts, including layouts	56

Really looking

Quiet poems: 1	explore how particular words are used, including words and expressions with similar meanings	57
Quiet poems: 2	explore how particular words are used, including words and expressions with similar meanings	58
Words and pictures	explore how particular words are used	59
Rough or smooth	explore how particular words are used	60

Silly stuff

Wild words	explore how particular words are used and compose descriptive phrases	61
A funny little man	explore how particular words are used in a nonsense rhyme	62
Mrs Brown went to town	explore how particular words are used in a nonsense rhyme	63
Tongue-twister match-up	explore how particular words are used in tongue-twisters	64

Introduction

100% New Developing Literacy Understanding and Responding to Texts is a series of seven photocopiable activity books for developing children's responses to different types of text and their understanding of the structure and purposes of different types of text.

The books provide learning activities to support strands 7 and 8 (Understanding and interpreting texts and Engaging with and responding to texts) of the literacy objectives of the Primary Framework for Literacy and Mathematics.

The structure of *100% New Developing Literacy Understanding and Responding to Texts: Ages 6–7* complements the structure and includes the range of text types suggested in the planning of the Primary Framework for children aged 6–7. It focuses on the following types of text:

- Narrative (stories with familiar settings, traditional stories, different stories by the same author, extended stories by significant children's authors)
- Non-fiction (instructions, explanations, information texts, non-chronological reports)
- Poetry (patterns on the page, really looking, silly stuff).

100% New Developing Literacy Understanding and Responding to Texts: Ages 6–7 addresses the following learning objectives from the Primary Framework for Literacy:

Strand 7 Understanding and interpreting texts

- Draw together ideas and information from across a whole text, using simple signposts in the text.
- Give some reasons why things happen or characters change.
- Explain organisational features of texts, including alphabetical order, layout, diagrams, captions, hyperlinks and bullet points.
- Use syntax and context to build their store of vocabulary when reading for meaning.
- Explore how particular words are used, including words and expressions with similar meanings.

Strand 8 Engaging with and responding to texts

- Read whole books on their own, choosing and justifying selections.
- Engage with books through exploring and enacting interpretations.
- Explain their reactions to texts, commenting on important aspects.

The activities

Some activities can be carried out with the whole class, some are more suitable for small groups and others are for individual work. It is important that the children have opportunities to listen to, repeat, learn, recite and join in stories and rhymes for enjoyment. Many of the activities can be adapted for use at different levels, to suit the differing levels of attainment of the children (see the Teachers' notes on the pages). Several can be used in different ways as explained in the *Notes on the activities* (see page 6).

Reading

Most children will be able to carry out the activities independently. It is not expected that the children should be able to read all the instructions on the sheets, but that someone will read them to or with them. The children gradually become accustomed to seeing instructions, and learn their purpose long before they can read them.

Organisation

The activities require very few resources besides pencils, crayons, scissors and glue. Other materials are specified in the Teachers' notes on the pages: for example, fiction, poetry or information books.

Extension activities

Most of the activity sheets end with a challenge (*Now try this!*) which reinforces and extends the children's learning and provides the teacher with an opportunity for assessment. These more challenging activities might be appropriate for only a few children; it is not expected that the whole  class should complete them, although many more children might benefit from them with appropriate assistance – possibly as a guided or shared activity. On some pages there is space for the children to complete the extension activities, but others will require a notebook or a separate sheet of paper.

Accompanying CD

The enclosed CD-ROM contains all the activity sheets from the book and allows you to edit them for printing or saving. This means that modifications can be made to further differentiate the activities to suit individual pupils' needs. See page 12 for further details.

Notes on the activities

The notes below expand upon those which are provided at the bottom of most activity pages. They give ideas and suggestions for making the most of the activity sheet, including suggestions for the whole-class introduction, the plenary session or for follow-up work using an adapted version of the activity sheet. To help teachers to select appropriate learning experiences for their pupils, the activities are grouped into sections within each book but the pages need not be presented in the order in which they appear, unless stated otherwise.

Stories and poems featured or suggested in this book and supplementary texts

Traditional tales:
Little Red Riding Hood, *Snow White and the Seven Dwarfs*, *Hansel and Gretel*, *Goldilocks and the Three Bears*, *Jack and the Beanstalk*, *Cinderella*, *The Sleeping Beauty*, *Rapunzel*, *The Gingerbread Man* (all Ladybird Books)

More modern stories:
Granny's Jungle Garden (Colin West, A & C Black), *Amazing Grace* (Mary Hoffman, Frances Lincoln), *Leon and Bob* (Simon James, Walker Books), *See you at the Match* (Margaret Joy, Faber & Faber), *Jessy and the Bridesmaid's Dress* (Rachel Anderson & Shelagh McNicholas, Young Lions *Jets* series, HarperCollins)

Extended stories by significant children's authors:
A Necklace of Raindrops (Joan Aiken, Puffin), *The Little Mermaid* (Hans Christian Andersen, Bluestar)

Useful books of poems and rhymes:
Poems for the Very Young (selected by Michael Rosen, Kingfisher), *The Puffin Book of Fantastic First Poems* (edited by June Crebbin, Puffin), *The Hutchinson Treasury of Children's Poetry* (edited by Alison Sage, Hutchinson), *Days Like This* (a collection of small poems by Simon James, Walker Books), *A Very First Poetry Book* (OUP), *Another Very First Poetry Book* (OUP)

Useful websites

Dual-language books:
http://www.kingston.gov.uk/browse/leisure/libraries/childrens_library_service/dual_language.htm

Selected fiction and non-fiction books and book boxes:
http://www.badger-publishing.co.uk/,
http://www.madeleinelindley.com/aboutus.aspx

Fairytales:
http://www.bbc.co.uk/cbeebies/storycircle/fairystories/
http://fairy-tales.classic-literature.co.uk/ (online text)
http://www.teachernet.gov.uk/teachingandlearning/library/fairytales/

Stories by significant children's authors:
http://hca.gilead.org.il/li_merma.html
www.andersen.sdu.dk/vaerk/hersholt/TheLittleMermaid_e.html
http://classiclit.about.com/library/bl-etexts/hcanderson/bl-hc anderson-mermaid.htm (*The Little Mermaid*, Hans Andersen)

http://www.ukchildrensbooks.co.uk/ (UK Book Directory of children's books)
http://www.strongest-links.org.uk/reading_authors.htm (children's authors)
http://www.randomhouse.co.uk/childrens/katiemorag/home.htm (Mairi Hedderwick)

Red squirrels:
http://www.forestry.gov.uk/forestry/Redsquirrel
http://www.saveoursquirrels.org.uk/red-squirrel-information/for children
http://ngfl.northumberland.gov.uk/ict/AAA/ukwild.htm
http://www.enchantedlearning.com/subjects/mammals/rodent/Squirrelprintout.shtml

Islands – Coll:
http://www.scottish-island-shopping.com/coll/vtour/
http://www.visitcoll.co.uk/
http://www.sturgeon.dircon.co.uk/AboutColl.htm
http://www.visitcoll.co.uk/images.php
http://www.scotland-info.co.uk/coll.htm

Poetry:
http://www.readwritethink.org/materials/shape/ (writing a shape poem)
http://atschool.eduweb.co.uk/sirrobhitch.suffolk/schoolwork/poetry/shape_poems/shape_poems.htm (children's shape poems)

Fiction
Stories in familiar settings

The activities in this section are about stories set in a familiar place, such as the home, school or neighbourhood, with themes that are familiar to the children: for example, wanting something and having to try hard for it, making a new friend, moving house, imaginary friends, visiting grandparents. The children are encouraged to think about the characters' feelings and how each character affects the others and the events of the story and to consider how the choices they make affect what happens.

Sad to say (page 13) helps the children to consider story structure, identify the main and other characters and consider how they affect one another's feelings and the events of the story. Also encourage them to give reasons why events happen and, where applicable, what makes characters change in a story they have read or listened to. Suitable stories include: *See you at the Match* by Margaret Joy (Faber & Faber) (or the extract entitled *The Autograph* in *The Kingfisher Treasury of Stories for Seven Year Olds*), about a boy who breaks his leg and cannot go to the football match; and *Jessy and the Bridesmaid's Dress* by Rachel Anderson & Shelagh McNicholas (Young Lions *Jets* series, HarperCollins), about a girl with Downs' Syndrome who wants to be a bridesmaid and is sad because her teacher is leaving the school when she gets married.

Granny's Jungle Garden (page 14) is based on a familiar experience for many children – visiting their grandmother, in this case a grandmother whose garden is a wilderness, but a paradise for wildlife. The children learn to identify characters and to describe them, in particular from how they behave and so on. A further extension activity could be to tell the story from Mr Smart's point of view. You could also link this with work on adjectives: ask the children to suggest words to describe each character (for example, *neat, tidy, fussy, happy, cheerful*).

Amazing Grace (page 15) is based on *Amazing Grace* by Mary Hoffman (Frances Lincoln) and is set in a familiar environment (school). It focuses on the feelings, personality and talents of the main character, Grace. You could stop at various points in the story and ask how Grace feels and what she might do. Ask which characters helped her. This could be linked with work in citizenship on Taking part and Living in a diverse world: issues of racism and equal opportunities could be discussed at a simple level (Can a girl play the part of Peter Pan? Is there any reason why Grace, who is black, cannot play this part?). The children could look for examples to show why Grace would be good in this role (she is good at acting and will work hard at it).

Leon and Bob **story map** (page 16) encourages the children to engage with books through exploring interpretations and to explain their reactions to texts. It also develops skills in identifying the main events of a story and retelling them in the correct order. As with the previous activities you could also draw out how the main character felt at different points in the story and how his imaginary friend Bob and real friend Bob helped.

Feelings (page 17) helps the children to notice words in the text which tell them how a character is feeling. You could base this on characters in the same story or different stories by the same author. Point out the verbs used instead of *said* and ask the children what they tell the reader about the character's feelings. Discuss which of the feelings could be used to describe more than one person: for example, *excited* could be used for Runa and Sam. The children could then look for similar examples in other books and highlight them in photocopies of the texts or in extracts on the interactive whiteboard or record them in a table. Encourage them to use these words in their own writing. This activity provides opportunities for children to read sentences aloud, using appropriate expression.

Traditional stories

These activities are based on traditional stories, including fairytales. They build on the children's previous learning and their knowledge of fairytale characters and provide opportunities for improvising on the stories and adding characters.

Character match (page 18) is about the characters in traditional tales. If appropriate, one or two characters and their descriptions could be omitted. Alternatively, some children

might be able to make additional picture and description cards based on other stories.

What if...? (page 19) provides an opportunity to consider an alternative version of the fairytale *The Sleeping Beauty* by changing the main character to a boy. Ask the children if the good fairies would give the same 'gifts' and what bad 'gift' the wicked fairy might give. How would these change the story? Also discuss how the title of the story might be changed.

Faces (page 20) encourages the children to consider how the illustrations of story characters affect what they think about them. Discuss how reliable it is to judge by appearances: for example, the beautiful but wicked queen in *Snow White and the Seven Dwarfs*. You could use this as an introduction to children describing and illustrating characters in their own stories.

That's not right (page 21) focuses on the effects of illustrations in storybooks and encourages the children to talk about what illustrations tell them about the story. Here the text does not match the picture. It provides an opportunity to review the children's learning about traditional story openings.

Let's ask Rapunzel (page 22) provides support for a 'hot-seating' activity in which children take the 'hot seat' as Rapunzel and the others ask them questions. You could encourage them to explore why the witch kept Rapunzel in a tower, what and how Rapunzel learned (she didn't go to school), the songs she sang, what she wore, what she could see from the window in the tower and so on. The children will be able to answer some of the questions using what they know from the story. For other questions, they will have to use what they know about the characters in the story to make their answers seem possible. This sheet can serve as a model for the children's own sheets about other characters.

Different stories by the same author

These activities help the children to notice the kinds of characters and settings an author writes about and to begin to learn about an author's style. The activities are generic and could be applied to any author's work.

Character quest (page 23) helps the children to focus on aspects of a character created by an author about whom they are learning. You could copy this page and display it on an interactive whiteboard; invite the children to add information in text boxes or on 'stickies'. Encourage the others to question this information; they could ask 'How do you know?' and those who wrote it could supply evidence from the story. Also discuss what they are not told in the story but can guess or imagine – and ask for evidence to support these guesses. Ask the children to think about whether the character changes during the story and, if so, in what ways. This kind of format can help with the children's own writing and creation of characters.

Book log (page 24) provides a framework on which to record information about books by an author. The children could complete each line as they finish reading a book by the author, and use the notes to help them to prepare a presentation about a book by the same author.

About the author (page 25) encourages the children to find out about a particular author. Prepare for this by setting up a display about the author: publishers' posters, posters and advertisements of films made about his or her stories, photographs, books he or she has written, books and articles about him or her. Point out sources of information about the author: books, posters, book-jacket blurbs and websites (publishers' and the author's own). The children could also look out for the author's books during library visits. As part of this work, they could write to or email the author, having checked whether he or she is still alive.

Extended stories by significant children's authors

> Several of these activities are generic and could be applied to any author or text; others feature specific significant authors: one from the past (Hans Christian Andersen) and one modern author (Joan Aiken). A long story could be selected to read with the children as a serial story while other long stories by the same author could be presented in a display, along with posters and information about the author to encourage independent reading.

Story tracker (page 26) helps the children to identify the main events of a story by a significant children's author. After reading each chapter of a story, encourage them to summarise the chapter and to say which was the most important event.

Reasons (page 27) focuses on identifying and explaining events in a story by a significant children's author: *A Necklace of Raindrops* by Joan Aiken (Puffin). It can be linked with work on questions. The children are required to think about the characters and events in the story and to say why they happened. It is useful to draw out common story themes, such as characters repaying help and kindness in the past when those who helped *them* face problems, and seemingly powerless characters, such as a fish, a bird and a mouse, having the power to overcome evil and affect the course of events.

Cliffhanger (page 28) presents a key moment in a story by a significant children's author (*The Little Mermaid* by Hans Christian Andersen) and encourages the children to predict what might happen next. You could focus on clues in the passage: for example, the only characters mentioned are the Little Mermaid and the young prince; in many stories a young girl falls in love with a prince and marries him. Also the prince is in danger as his ship is tossed by a storm, whereas the Little Mermaid is used to storms and is quite at home in any sea conditions.

Character clues (page 29) develops the children's skills in deducing what characters are like from descriptions and from recounts of their actions. Help them to use details in the passage to form an opinion of a character. At a simple level, they could decide whether the character is good or bad and then say what is good and what is bad about him or her. Ask them to use at least one word from the word-bank to describe each character.

The story judge (page 30) provides a format to help the children to record their opinions of a story. Ask them to think about how the setting is presented, what they liked or disliked about the characters, and parts of the story. Did the opening 'grab' them and make them want to read on? Did they find it interesting or exciting? Was it a good story? Ask them if it had a happy or a sad ending and which they would have preferred.

Non-fiction
Instructions

> These activities develop the children's understanding of the structure of sentences which give instructions and to distinguish between them and recount or descriptive sentences.

Hide and seek (page 31) develops skills in reading and following instructions. The children find where the gnomes are hiding in the picture. They could talk in their groups about how good the instructions were. Give them the solutions and ask them if they found these places. You could link this with work on word reading strategies (silent 'g').

Ladybird program (page 32) is about reading and following precise instructions. It links with work in ICT on programmable toys. The children could also work in pairs with one acting as instructor and the other acting as the robot that follows the instructions. Ask the children to notice the first word of each instruction (*Go*) and compare this with other instructions they have read. They could compile a list of instruction words: for example, *sit, turn, wait, stop*. Copy the grid onto card and provide ladybird cut-outs for children to move according to the instructions.

Stripy lolly (page 33) provides a recipe for the children to follow. It reinforces their previous learning that a recipe tells the reader how to make something and helps them to appreciate the use of diagrams in making instructions clear. Remind them how this is different from a story, in which the sentences say what happened. Also discuss how the sentences are different from captions. Link this with work in design and technology on healthy eating. The children could add explanations to the instructions: for example, why the top colour is poured into the yogurt pot first and is at the bottom of the pot (the diagram helps). They could add 'so that' or 'because' clauses to the instruction sentences.

Simon says (page 34) demonstrates the difference between describing what someone is doing and giving an instruction.

You could first play 'Simon says' with the children. Ask them what Simon is doing in the first picture. Repeat their answer as a sentence, and then ask them what Simon would say in the game 'Simon says'. Draw out the difference between this instruction and the sentence which said what he was doing. Ask the children to write what he says in the speech bubble. Remind them that they should not write 'Simon says' and point out that Simon is giving instructions – he is telling someone what to do. Link this with sentence work on quotations and speech marks.

Explanations

Here the activities concentrate on texts which explain a process, using diagrams where appropriate.

Dragon life cycle (page 35) develops the children's skills in using diagrams in explanations. Ask them to think about why the life of an animal or plant is called a 'life cycle'. You could ask them where they have heard the word *cycle* used. Ask them what came first – the dragon or the egg. If they say 'the egg', ask where it came from and draw out that the dragon that laid it came from an egg. A group of six children could each hold an enlarged copy of a stage of the dragon's life cycle and arrange themselves in the correct order. If they arrange themselves in a straight line, help them to make links between the two ends of the line so that they form a circle. You could draw a life cycle diagram (copy and enlarge the one at the top of the page) onto which the children can glue the pictures. Before the children cut out the pictures on the sheet, discuss the instructions for the activity. Why do they think that bullet points have been used? How do they help to make the instructions easier to follow? Why aren't the captions on the cards whole sentences? In the plenary session, ask the children how the diagram makes it easier to understand what happens in a dragon's life.

Fairyland (page 36) is about the features of information texts. The children use notes presented in a fact-file to help them to complete a cloze passage about fairies. Draw out how this is different from a fairytale, which is a story about what happened. The fact-file can help to answer the question at the top of the page; information texts help us to find things out.

Buildings glossary: 1 and **2** (pages 37–38) helps the children to understand the structure of a glossary and how to use it. Introduce or revise the term *definition* and ask the children to cut out the definitions and the pictures with their captions. The cards can be used in various ways: for example, give each child a picture with a caption and then read definitions at random. The child with the picture and caption that match the definition puts up a hand to claim it. Ask each group to put their definitions in alphabetical order. If appropriate, you could then give the entire set to a group to put in alphabetical order. Discuss why a glossary is arranged in alphabetical order and how this helps. Demonstrate this by asking different groups to locate a definition in an alphabetically ordered glossary and a randomly organised glossary.

Information texts

This section is about using non-fiction texts to find information through using contents pages, menus and alphabetical order: scanning to find specific sections, skimming to find information and close reading to find details.

Miss Muffet's friends (page 39) helps the children to understand the structure of an alphabetically ordered text and how to use it. Explain that names are usually listed by family name rather than personal name. Some children might need to use an alphabet strip and to match the names to the letters. They could also make their own address books and enter the names and addresses of their friends. Link this with work on capital letters and with work in geography on streets, towns, countries and different kinds of maps.

Fairytale facts (page 40) helps the children to use an alphabetically ordered text to find information. Some of them could also enter the names of their class (or a section of the class on a table in Word) and use the 'Sort' command in the menu to put them in order. Ask them how it sorted those beginning with the same letter. You could also provide a random list of words and an alphabetically ordered list and let the children investigate which is the easier to use. They could write their full names on slips of paper and arrange them in alphabetical order of personal name and then family name.

Look it up (page 41) helps the children to use the alphabetically ordered text of a dictionary to find information to answer questions. You could mask some of the questions to make the activity less challenging. Different groups could use different dictionaries and, in the plenary session, compare the definitions.

Book skimmer (page 42) provides practice in skim-reading books in order to ascertain whether they contain the information that is wanted. Read the terms highlighted in boxes with the children and ask them to point these out in information books. Model how to use these to find out what is in a book without reading all of it.

Web skimmer (page 43) provides practice in skim-reading website home pages in order to ascertain whether they contain the information that is wanted. Read the terms highlighted in boxes with the children and ask them to point these out on website home pages. Model how to use these to find out what is on a website without reading every page. See the list on page 6 for suggestions of websites to use for this activity.

Answer finder (page 44) provides practice in scanning a passage from a text in order to locate specific information. Look at a question with the children and model how to read quickly, picking out key words and phrases. Provide different information books for different groups and, during the plenary session, invite them to compare the information they found. Also compare the different ways in which it is presented and ask the children which they like the best: labelled diagrams, charts, solid text, photographs or drawings with captions.

Seashore scanner (page 45) provides practice in skim-reading a text to find the parts that will help to answer a question and then scanning these to locate specific information to fill gaps in a cloze passage. Model how to skim a book to check whether it contains the information you need and then how to scan a page to find more detail. For a less challenging version of the activity, provide a word-bank: *cockle, cormorant, crabs, dead, eight, hermit, kittiwake, mussel, new, sand, seaweed, skeletons*. The children could look up these words in the index of information books. Examples of books you could use for this activity are: *DK Pop-Up Deep Blue Sea* (Dorling Kindersley), *Usborne Spotter's Guides The Seashore* (Usborne), *Collins Gem Seashore* (Collins). This could be linked with work in science.

Non-chronological reports

> The activities in this section develop skills in selecting, scanning and skimming information books and reading non-chronological reports in different media to find information and the answers to questions. They link with work in other subjects. The first three complement work in geography (An island home), one is based on a history topic (The Gunpowder Plot), one links with work in science (Materials) and the other is generic.

Island reports (page 46) is about using different types of information text to find out about an island. It focuses on literacy skills in the context of geography (An island home). Choose an island to investigate (e.g. Coll, see below) and collect a leaflet or travel brochure, a book and details of a website. Show the children the three texts and ask them how they are similar. Ask them what is different about them: for example, the amount of text and pictures, how to find pages, the number of pages, how they are set out: where the headings, pictures, diagrams and captions are arranged. Show them how to locate the contents/menu of each text (if it has one) and ask them what they think they will find in the text: for example, photographs of the island, sound recordings, videos, panoramic views, interactive quizzes. During the plenary session, ask the children which text they enjoyed using the most and what they liked about it and which was the most useful, and why. This activity could be linked with reading the Katie Morag stories by Mairi Hedderwick (Random House), set on the imaginary island of Struay (based on the author's home on the island of Coll in the Hebrides). See page 6 which lists useful websites about Coll. Other websites you could use are: http://www.isle-of-man.com/, http://www.iwight.com/, http://www.lindisfarne.org.uk/ and http://www.visitanglesey.com/.

Island fact-file (page 47) develops from the activity on page 46. Having discovered what a website contains, the children use it to find specific information. Model how to scan the menu or site map and 'think aloud' about the headings and pictures and whether they will provide information about the landscape, coast and buildings: for example, 'This button says Shoreline. That means coast, so it will tell me about the seashores around the island. It might even show pictures of them.' The children could use books or brochures to find the same information and say which they found the easiest, and why.

Key words map (page 48) is about preparing to find information from non-fiction books and websites. It develops from pages 46–47 as it focuses on a specific aspect of an island (tourism).The children begin by making notes on a concept map about what they know or think will be useful to visitors to an island. They can then use information texts to find out more about each heading: for example, names and locations of hotels and other accommodation.

Guy Fawkes information race: 1 and **2** (pages 49–50) help the children to compare two information texts about the same topic through taking part in a 'race' to complete a quiz. They could work in two teams or as individuals. Useful resources about Guy Fawkes include: http://www.bonfire.org/guy/ and http://www.guyfawkes.me.uk/; *Who Was Guy Fawkes?* by Dereen Taylor (Hodder Wayland), *The Life of Guy Fawkes* by Emma Lynch (Heinemann Library) and *Guy Fawkes (Famous People, Famous Lives)* by Harriet Castor and Peter Kent (Franklin Watts). During the plenary session, compare the results. Which teams were the fastest? Discuss whether it is quicker and easier to use a website or a book. When the children complete page 50, ask them to talk to their groups about what they liked and disliked about each text and what made it easy or difficult to use.

Note it (page 51) develops skills in making and reading notes. The chart provides a model for note-making. It could be adapted for recording other investigations in science. The emphasis here is on interpreting a chart in order to find information to answer questions. Point out the key and, if necessary, explain it. As an extension activity the children could write another question for a friend to answer using the chart. You could write questions for the children to answer using notes they have made on a chart about another investigation.

Poetry
Patterns on the page

> Here the children read and explore a selection of poems with different patterned structures and experiment with the patterns, adding their own words, lines or verses.

Sea song (page 52) is about rhyming patterns and repeated language. After reading the first verse and the first two lines of the second verse, the children should realise that each verse begins *Sea-shell, sea-shell*, and that this is followed by a line which is repeated (*Murmuring sand, Murmuring sand*) and that in each verse these two lines rhyme with *sand*: *land, hand, understand*. Read the entire poem, stopping for the children to continue where there is a gap. They could later make up their own poems based on this structure, beginning, for example, with *Seagull, seagull, Cries in the air, Cries in the air*.

Anna Elise (page 53) encourages the children to explore the structure of an action poem. It provides an opportunity for reading and responding to a poem that invites action, practising and reading a poem in unison, following the rhythm, keeping time and exploring and emphasising the pattern. The children can imitate and invent actions while reading the poem. Encourage them to look at the pictures and then enact them. You could help the children to develop their sense of the pattern – a word ending one line then becoming the focus of the next. They could circle each repeated noun and join them: *surprise, surprise, chair, chair*. They could also make up their own additional verses, ensuring that Anna Elise ends up turning around. Other useful rhyming words include: *low/slow/snow/crow, ice/nice/twice, more/door/floor, flat/hat/mat/cat, big/wig/pig, high/dry/sky/fly/pie, wavy/gravy/navy*.

Fire! Fire! (page 54) consolidates the children's appreciation of rhyme as they complete the sentences with names that rhyme with the words people say. They should also notice the structure and pattern of the poem: it is in the form of a dialogue – each person responds to the words of the previous speaker and these are arranged in logical pairs: observation/response. The children are asked to make up their own rhyming verses based on the poem, with starting points provided.

Bouncing (page 55) focuses on the rhythm of a child bouncing on a bed – 'Bouncing' by Simon James (in *Days Like This*, Simon James, Walker Books). It has a pattern which mimics children bouncing on a bed as they talk about what they are doing – this monologue is punctuated by bounces. You could begin by reading the poem twice – first in a very straightforward way and then in a breathless way as if you are bouncing.

Shape match (page 56) develops the children's learning about the effect of the layout of a poem on the page, through introducing shape poems. They develop an appreciation of how this affects the way in which they read the poem. Ask them to look at the shapes and to say the word which first comes to mind. Can they match this to one of the poems?

Really looking

> The activities in this section provide opportunities for the children to read and respond to poems based on closely observed experience, focusing on adventurous language, effectively used and which does not necessarily contain rhyme or conform to any poetic form.

Quiet poems: 1 and **2** (pages 57–58) present two poems about lying in bed at night, listening. The first has no rhyme. It has a very slow, gentle pace; the words and their layout urge the reader to read slowly and quietly. The second poem has some rhyme but no regular rhyming pattern. The effect is to slow the reading, as for the first poem. Encourage the children to notice the sounds which occur the most often in these two poems: *s, z* and *sh* (*stars, switched, still, sleeping, except; shhhhhhhhh*,

eyelashes, stroking, breeze, whispers, trees) and *l* (*listen, lie, still, sleeping, eyelashes*).

Words and pictures (page 59) encourages awareness of the pictures a poem conjures up in the mind. The focus is on how sounds can create images such as a beating drum, a fast-moving train, a tiptoeing child and whizzing and whooshing fireworks. Some children will be able to complete the extension activity independently; for others this could be a shared writing activity. You could provide a video recording of an event with noticeable sounds and rhythm: part of a football match, playtime at school, waves crashing onto a shore, a horse galloping, birds flying, bees buzzing around flowers and so on. Ask the children to suggest words to describe the pictures they see: write these in a word-bank and add some of your own.

Rough or smooth (page 60) focuses on the quality of sounds. It helps the children to appreciate how the sounds of words can create an effect. Other words to consider include: *clatter, crash, flashing, flow, glide, luminous, ragged, snag*.

Silly stuff

> This section is about playing with words to create poems which need have no sensible meaning, although they might be jokes. It encourages the children to play with words and enjoy their sounds as well as to explore plays on words.

Wild words (page 61) is about describing words. As the children complete it, encourage them to read the phrases aloud, to listen to the sounds of the words and to imagine the pictures they conjure up.

A funny little man (page 62) provides an opportunity to have fun with a nonsense rhyme and to enjoy its silliness. Discuss the rhyming pattern: end rhyme, then internal rhyme. The children could highlight these parts of the first verse to help them to recognise the pattern. They could make up their own verses during any spare moments. Let them explore these with a friend and recite them to the class.

Mrs Brown went to town (page 63) presents a silly story/song. Sing it with the children and let them sing it with a friend and improvise on the verses or add their own. The only rule to follow is to keep to the rhyming pattern and the rhythm (you could show the children how to count the beats or syllables of the lines) and that the new verses have to be nonsense. They will also have to make up names for the last line.

Tongue-twister match-up (page 64) develops an appreciation of alliteration. After the children have matched up the two parts of each tongue-twister, ask them to read it aloud quickly. Can they do so without making a mistake? They could create lists of alliterative words and make up their own tongue-twisters.

Using the CD-ROM

The PC CD-ROM included with this book contains an easy-to-use software program that allows you to print out pages from the book, to view them (e.g. on an interactive whiteboard) or to customise the activities to suit the needs of your pupils.

Getting started

It's easy to run the software. Simply insert the CD-ROM into your CD drive and the disk should autorun and launch the interface in your web browser.

If the disk does not autorun, open 'My Computer' and select the CD drive, then open the file 'start.html'.

Please note: this CD-ROM is designed for use on a PC. It will also run on most Apple Macintosh computers in Safari however, due to the differences between Mac and PC fonts, you may experience some unavoidable variations in the typography and page layouts of the activity sheets.

The Menu screen

Four options are available to you from the main menu screen.

The first option takes you to the Activity Sheets screen, where you can choose an activity sheet to edit or print out using Microsoft Word.

(If you do not have the Microsoft Office suite, you might like to consider using OpenOffice instead. This is a multi-platform and multi-lingual office suite, and an 'open-source' project. It is compatible with all other major office suites, and the product is free to download, use and distribute. The homepage for OpenOffice on the Internet is: www.openoffice.org.)

The second option on the main menu screen opens a PDF file of the entire book using Adobe Reader (see below). This format is ideal for printing out copies of the activity sheets or for displaying them, for example on an interactive whiteboard.

The third option allows you to choose a page to edit from a text-only list of the activity sheets, as an alternative to the graphical interface on the Activity Sheets screen.

Adobe Reader is free to download and to use. If it is not already installed on your computer, the fourth link takes you to the download page on the Adobe website.

You can also navigate directly to any of the three screens at any time by using the tabs at the top.

The Activity Sheets screen

This screen shows thumbnails of all the activity sheets in the book. Rolling the mouse over a thumbnail highlights the page number and also brings up a preview image of the page.

Click on the thumbnail to open a version of the page in Microsoft Word (or an equivalent software program, see above.) The full range of editing tools are available to you here to customise the page to suit the needs of your particular pupils. You can print out copies of the page or save a copy of your edited version onto your computer.

The Index screen

This is a text-only version of the Activity Sheets screen described above. Choose an activity sheet and click on the 'download' link to open a version of the page in Microsoft Word to edit or print out.

Technical support

If you have any questions regarding the *100% New Developing Literacy* or *Developing Mathematics* software, please email us at the address below. We will get back to you as quickly as possible.

educationalsales@acblack.com

Sad to say

Story title

Story title

_____

- **Draw and name the** characters .
- **Write in their speech bubbles.**

Main character

I was sad because _____

_____

_____

_____

Name _____

Another character

This is how I helped.

_____

_____

_____

Name _____

NOW TRY THIS!

- **Tell the story with a friend.**
- **Show how the characters feel.**

Teachers' note Use this to help the children to focus on the response of a story character to a problem, mishap or other major event in a story and how another character interacts with him or her. Reread parts of the story and ask how the character felt. Ask the children what happened to make him or her feel better, who helped, and how.

100% New Developing Literacy
Understanding and Responding
to Texts: Ages 6–7
© A & C BLACK

13

Granny's Jungle Garden

Granny's garden is full of tall plants and long grass.

Mr Smart's garden is very neat.

Granny's Jungle Garden is a story by Colin West.

- **Who does this?**
- **Write** Granny **or** Mr Smart .

mows the lawn every Friday

cuts the hedge every Tuesday

sits listening to the insects buzzing

sprays the plants with insect killer

feeds the birds

sits listening to the birds singing

brushes the lawn

puts weedkiller on the lawn

NOW TRY THIS!

- **What might Granny and Mr Smart say to one another?**
- **Act this with a friend.**

Teachers' note Use this page with the story *Granny's Jungle Garden* by Colin West (A & C Black). Ask the children about the characters Granny and Mr Smart, focusing on any similarities (they both have gardens) and differences (Granny's garden is a wilderness but Mr Smart's is very tidy). They will probably remember, or be able to figure out, which statements apply to which character.

100% New Developing Literacy Understanding and Responding to Texts: Ages 6–7 © A & C BLACK

Amazing Grace

Grace loves stories.
She acts them out.
There is going to be a
pantomime at school.
Grace wants to be Peter Pan.
This is what some children say:

Amazing Grace is
a story by
Mary Hoffman.

You can't.
Peter Pan's
a boy.

Raj

You can't. Peter Pan
isn't black.

Natalie

• **Write what Grace said.**

NOW TRY THIS!

• **What will Grace do?**
  Will she be Peter Pan? How?
• **Tell the story.**

Teachers' note This is based on *Amazing Grace* by Mary Hoffman (Frances Lincoln). Ask the children to describe Grace; draw out what she is like, including her interest in, and talent for, acting. You could also talk about what made her sad and who helped, as for page 13.

100% New Developing Literacy
Understanding and Responding
to Texts: Ages 6–7
© A & C BLACK

Leon and Bob story map

- Leon and Bob is a story by Simon James.
- Retell the story using the pictures.

NOW TRY THIS!

- How did Leon change?
- Tell a friend what was different about Leon.

Teachers' note This is based on *Leon and Bob* by Simon James. The children can use the story map to help them to retell the story in their own words. Afterwards, encourage them to think about Leon's feelings at each stage and to tell the story in a way which expresses these.

100% New Developing Literacy
Understanding and Responding
to Texts: Ages 6–7
© A & C BLACK

Feelings

- **How do the characters feel ?**
- **Write in the boxes.**

"Over here!" screamed Runa.

[ ]

"We missed it," sighed Jan.

[ ]

"We missed it," growled Lee.

[ ]

Word-bank

angry

disappointed

excited

frightened

happy

pleased

"What a goal!" exclaimed Sam.

[ ]

"Look at that!" whispered Mick, trembling.

[ ]

"Look at that!" smiled Dan.

[ ]

NOW TRY THIS!

- **Underline the words that give you a clue to how the characters feel.**

Teachers' note After reading a section of a story in which characters' feelings are communicated through what they say, and how, ask the children how the character felt and how they could tell. Focus on words which express how they speak, as well as discussing what they say and how they have changed.

100% New Developing Literacy
Understanding and Responding
to Texts: Ages 6–7
© A & C BLACK

Character match

• **Match the** descriptions **to the pictures.**

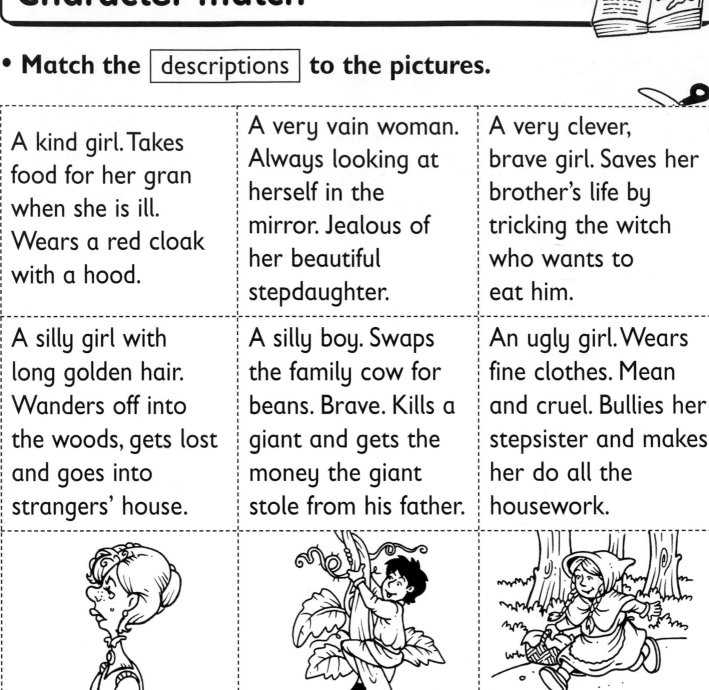

A kind girl. Takes food for her gran when she is ill. Wears a red cloak with a hood.

A very vain woman. Always looking at herself in the mirror. Jealous of her beautiful stepdaughter.

A very clever, brave girl. Saves her brother's life by tricking the witch who wants to eat him.

A silly girl with long golden hair. Wanders off into the woods, gets lost and goes into strangers' house.

A silly boy. Swaps the family cow for beans. Brave. Kills a giant and gets the money the giant stole from his father.

An ugly girl. Wears fine clothes. Mean and cruel. Bullies her stepsister and makes her do all the housework.

Ugly Sister

Jack

Red Riding Hood

Wicked Queen

Goldilocks

Gretel

Teachers' note Glue this page onto card and cut out the character descriptions and pictures. These can be used in various ways: the children could take turns to read out a character description and the others could look for the matching picture; you could give some children a picture card and others a description, and ask them to find their partners; or they could play 'matching pairs'.

100% New Developing Literacy Understanding and Responding to Texts: Ages 6–7
© A & C BLACK

What if...?

The King and Queen invited all the fairies to see the baby.

- **What if the baby had been a boy?**
- **Write what the good fairies would have said.**
- **Write what the bad fairy would have said.**

NOW TRY THIS!

- **What might happen next?**
- **Talk to a friend about the story.**

Teachers' note This is based on the fairytale *The Sleeping Beauty*. Read the beginning of the story and use this page to help the children to retell the story so far and to imagine what might have happened if the baby had been a boy.

100% New Developing Literacy Understanding and Responding to Texts: Ages 6–7
© A & C BLACK

19

Faces

- **Look at the faces.**
- **Choose two words for each** | character |.

Teachers' note Ask the children if they can tell what a story character is like from pictures. They could discuss the faces on this page with a friend before they select words to describe him or her. Also discuss characters who look beautiful but are bad (for example, Snow White's wicked stepmother) and ugly characters who are good (for example, the Beast in *Beauty and the Beast*).

Word-bank

clever	mean
evil	nasty
fierce	nice
friendly	proud
funny	puzzled
gentle	silly
happy	vain
kind	wise

NOW TRY THIS!

- **Look at a picture of another character.**
- **Write a sentence about the character's face.**

100% New Developing Literacy
Understanding and Responding
to Texts: Ages 6–7
© A & C BLACK

That's not right

- **Change the story** [opening] **to match the picture.**

Once upon a time there was a little boy named Lee. He lived in a little hut in the woods with his mother, who was a washerwoman. They were very poor. They ate simple food and some days they had nothing at all to eat.

Once upon a time there was a _____ named

_____. _____ lived in a _____ in the woods

with _____, who was a _____.

They were very _____. They ate _____ food and

some days they had _____ to eat.

_____

_____

NOW TRY THIS!

- **Write two more sentences for the story opening.**

Teachers' note Introduce the term *opening* for the start of a story and ask the children for some typical opening words of fairytales. Use a storybook as an example to show how the illustrations help to set the scene, and then ask the children to read this story opening. Does it match the picture? Discuss which parts need to be changed. They should invent a name for the main character.

100% New Developing Literacy
Understanding and Responding
to Texts: Ages 6–7
© A & C BLACK

Let's ask Rapunzel

- **Read the children's questions.**
- **Write Rapunzel's answers.**

1 *What is in the tower?*

2 *What do you do apart from singing?*

3 *What did you do before the witch locked you in the tower?*

1

2

3

NOW TRY THIS!

- **Write another question for Rapunzel.**
- **Give it to a friend to answer.**

Teachers' note This could be used to prepare for or to follow up a 'hot-seating' activity in which a volunteer acts as Rapunzel and the others ask her questions about her past, what happened to her and why, and about other characters in the story. The children could first talk in pairs about the story and what they would like to ask Rapunzel.

**100% New Developing Literacy
Understanding and Responding
to Texts: Ages 6–7**
© A & C BLACK

Character quest

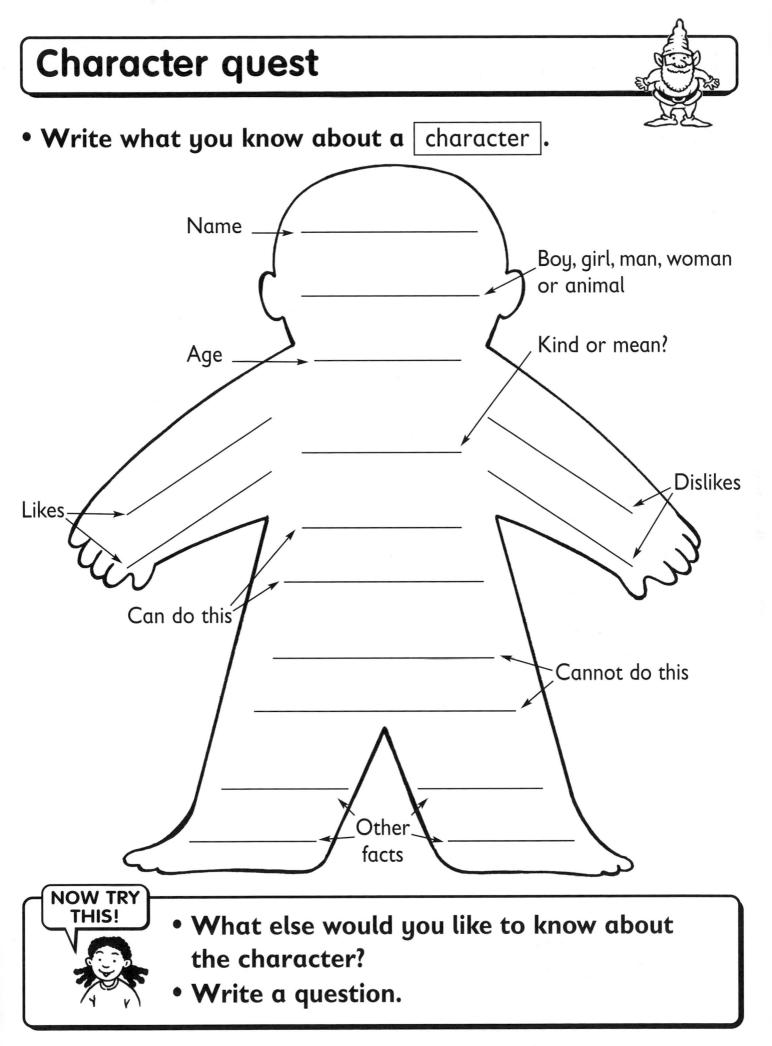

• **Write what you know about a** character .

Name

Boy, girl, man, woman or animal

Kind or mean?

Age

Dislikes

Likes

Can do this

Cannot do this

Other facts

NOW TRY THIS!

• **What else would you like to know about the character?**
• **Write a question.**

Teachers' note This page could support work on a character who appears in either one or several books by an author. Enlarge the page to A3 or display it on an interactive whiteboard to use it with a group. The character outline helps the children to record different aspects of the character in an organised way.

100% New Developing Literacy Understanding and Responding to Texts: Ages 6–7 © A & C BLACK

Book log

Name of [author] _____

Books I have read

Title	Characters	Setting	Important event

NOW TRY THIS!

- Which was your favourite book by this author?
- Tell a friend about the part you liked best.

100% New Developing Literacy
Understanding and Responding
to Texts: Ages 6–7
© A & C BLACK

Teachers' note This page should be used once the children have become familiar with an author. Encourage them to talk about their favourite books by this author and why they like them. They could use the book log to help them to prepare a talk to the rest of the class about what they have found out about the author.

About the author

Name of author _____

- **Glue or draw a picture of the author here.**

Where the author lives or lived
_____

Family
_____
_____

Pets
_____

Interests
_____

His or her favourite authors
_____

Other information
_____
_____
_____
_____

NOW TRY THIS!

- **Write a question you would like to ask the author.**
_____
_____

Teachers' note This is designed to support work on a specific author. First the author should be introduced: for example, through a display of books and posters and, if possible, listening to readings of sections of his or her books. This page provides a framework on which the children can record information they find about an author from book jacket blurbs, posters and websites.

100% New Developing Literacy
Understanding and Responding
to Texts: Ages 6–7
© A & C BLACK

Story tracker

- **Write notes about the** main events **in a story.**

Title _____ Author _____

Chapter [ ]

Chapter [ ]

Chapter [ ]

Chapter [ ]

Chapter [ ]

Chapter [ ]

Look at your notes before you read the next chapter.

NOW TRY THIS!

- **Use your notes to help you to retell the story.**

100% New Developing Literacy
Understanding and Responding
to Texts: Ages 6–7
© A & C BLACK

Teachers' note Use this to help the children to understand the structure of a longer story. You could enlarge the page to A3 to allow more space for writing. Model how to complete the first section by talking about the first chapter of the story and identifying the main events. Show the children how to make a note of these.

Reasons

Title <u>A Necklace of Raindrops</u>

Author <u>Joan Aiken</u>

- **Why did it happen?**
- **Write the** reason .

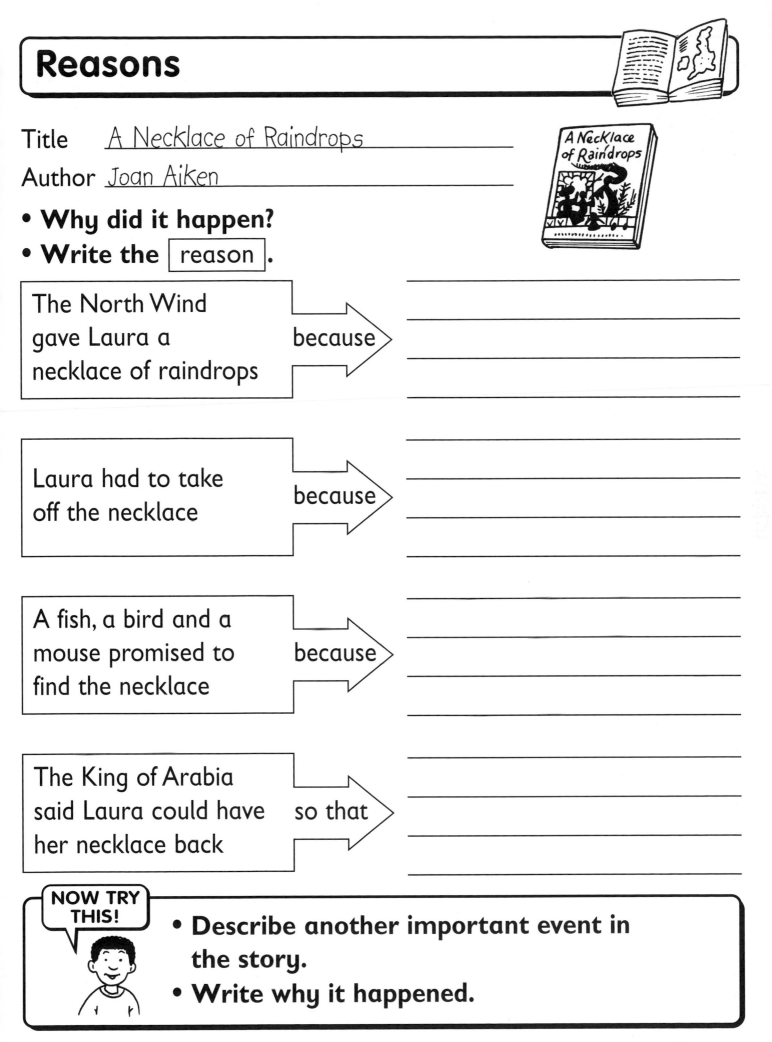

The North Wind gave Laura a necklace of raindrops	because	
Laura had to take off the necklace	because	
A fish, a bird and a mouse promised to find the necklace	because	
The King of Arabia said Laura could have her necklace back	so that	

NOW TRY THIS!

- **Describe another important event in the story.**
- **Write why it happened.**

Teachers' note This page supports discussion of the main events of a story, focusing on why they happened. You could use the software on the enclosed CD-ROM to adapt the sheet by blanking out part so that it can be used with another story (or copy it onto a whiteboard and use the eraser).

100% New Developing Literacy Understanding and Responding to Texts: Ages 6–7 © A & C BLACK

Cliffhanger

- **What might happen next?**
- **Write and draw on the notepad.**

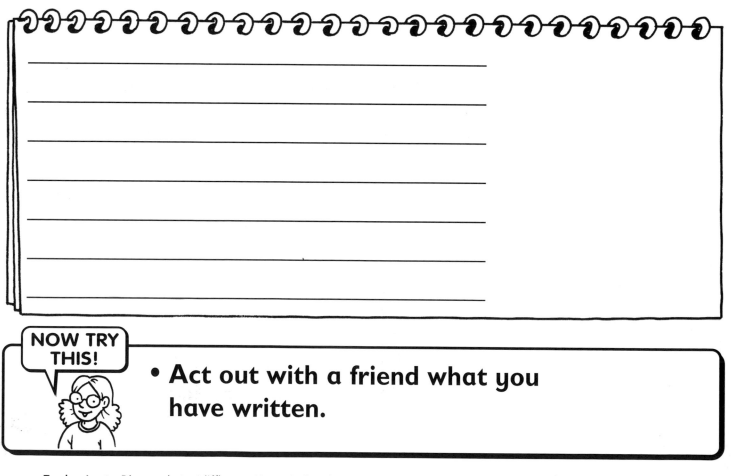

There was a ship on the calm sea. The little mermaid could hear music and singing. People danced on the decks, and a hundred coloured lanterns lit them up. The little mermaid swam close to the cabin windows and peered in. She could see a young prince with large black eyes. When he came on deck, more than a hundred rockets rose in the air. The sky became as bright as day. The little mermaid was so startled that she dived under the water. When she came up it seemed as if all the stars of heaven were falling around her. She had never seen fireworks before.

Then a moaning, grumbling sound came from beneath the waves. They rose higher, and heavy clouds filled the sky. The ship dived like a swan between the waves and then rose again on their lofty, foaming crests. To the little mermaid this was fun, but not to the sailors. Before long the ship groaned and creaked. The thick planks broke. The mast snapped like a reed, the ship lay on its side and the water rushed in.

Retold from *The Little Mermaid* by Hans Christian Andersen

NOW TRY THIS!

- **Act out with a friend what you have written.**

Teachers' note Discuss what a 'cliffhanger' is, and what the purpose of such moments is in stories. Whether or not the children have read or listened to *The Little Mermaid* by Hans Christian Andersen they will be able to enjoy this passage and to talk about the main character. Ask them which other character is introduced and what might connect the two characters.

100% New Developing Literacy Understanding and Responding to Texts: Ages 6–7 © A & C BLACK

Character clues

- **What are the** | characters | **like?**
- **Fill in the gaps.**

Mrs Smark stared at him from behind the counter.
Her top lip curled up at the side as she slid the parcel
across the table.

Mrs Smark is _____

Word-bank

brave   mean

evil   nasty

friendly   pleasant

good   scary

kind   sensible

Old Jim had a round face that reminded Ella of a big
red apple. His twinkling brown eyes danced as he
smiled at her.

Old Jim is _____

Mr Scratchit was scraping around in his garden as usual, muttering to himself. His
bony elbows poked out of holes in his jumper. I was glad I could only see the back
of him because his sharp, narrow, blue eyes scared me.

Mr Scratchit is _____

Nina rested her hand on Natalie's arm and looked at her gently. "Don't cry," she said.
"You can come and stay with us while your mum is in hospital. We'll look after you."

Nina is _____

Leo ran along the path through the field. The match was due to start in five minutes.
But what was that noise? It was coming from the pond. Maybe someone had fallen
in. Leo stepped though the long grass and pushed the bushes apart. There was the
pond. A hand and a head came up through the water. Leo had to act fast.

Leo is _____

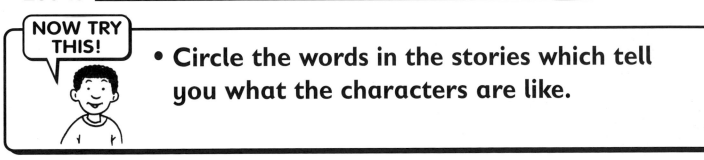

NOW TRY THIS!

- **Circle the words in the stories which tell
  you what the characters are like.**

Teachers' note Read the first passage with the children and invite comments about what Mrs
Smark is like. Encourage the children to say why they think this and to quote words from the text
which give them this impression. They could compare the passage with a description such as 'Mrs
Smark, the shopkeeper, was nasty.' Which helps them best to imagine Mrs Smark?

100% New Developing Literacy
**Understanding and Responding
to Texts: Ages 6–7**
© A & C BLACK

The story judge

Title _____

Author _____

Illustrator _____

Publisher _____

| Key | 😊 I like it very much | 😐 I think it is OK. | ☹️ I do not like it. |

• Fill in the chart.

		What I liked or disliked most about it
Setting	😐	
Main character	😐	
Other characters	😐	
Beginning	😐	
The story	😐	
Ending	😐	

NOW TRY THIS!

• **Write a report to tell others why they should or shouldn't read this story.**

Teachers' note Use this to help the children to record their responses to a story by a significant children's author. Different children could focus on different stories and present their responses to the class.

100% New Developing Literacy
Understanding and Responding
to Texts: Ages 6–7
© A & C BLACK

Hide and seek

- **Draw the gnome family in the picture.**
- **Colour them in.**

Norman Gnome
Follow the path until you come to a bridge.
Look under the bridge.

Norma Gnome
Follow the path.
Cross the bridge.
Keep on the path.
Look in the house.

Nora Gnome
Go to the tallest tree.
Cross the path.
Look behind the bushes.

Noah Gnome
Follow the path until you come to a fence.
Go through the gate.
Follow the path until you come to a pond.
Look in the boat.

START

NOW TRY THIS!

- **Hide something small.**
- **Write** instructions **for a friend to find it.**

a shell   a ball   a marble   a coin

Teachers' note Read the first piece of text with the children and help them to follow the instructions. Ask if they are good instructions. Point out that instructions tell the reader what they need and what they should do (in the correct order). The children can then read and follow the rest of the instructions.

100% New Developing Literacy
Understanding and Responding
to Texts: Ages 6–7
© A & C BLACK

Ladybird program

- **Read the** | instructions | **.**
- **Draw the ladybird in the correct square.**

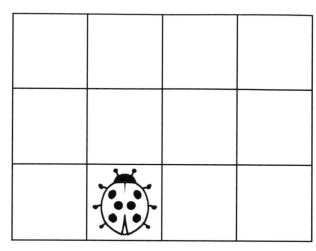

Go forward one square.

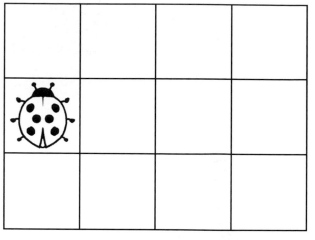

Go back one square.

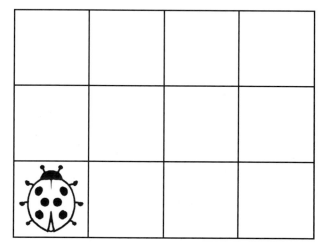

Go forward two squares.

Turn right.

Go forward one square.

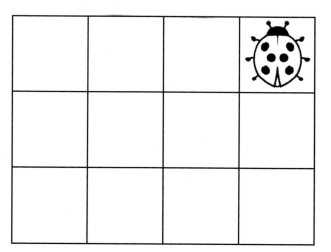

Go back one square.

Turn left.

Go forward three squares.

NOW TRY THIS!

- **Does the** | order | **of the instructions matter?**
- **Find out with a friend.**

Teachers' note Ensure that the children know which directions are meant by *forward, back, left* and *right*. You could write these on the page and add arrows to show the directions. Invite a volunteer to read the first instruction and to point out the square the ladybird will end on. The children can then draw the ladybird in this square and do the same for the subsequent instructions.

100% New Developing Literacy Understanding and Responding to Texts: Ages 6–7
© A & C BLACK

Stripy lolly

- **Fill in the gaps.**

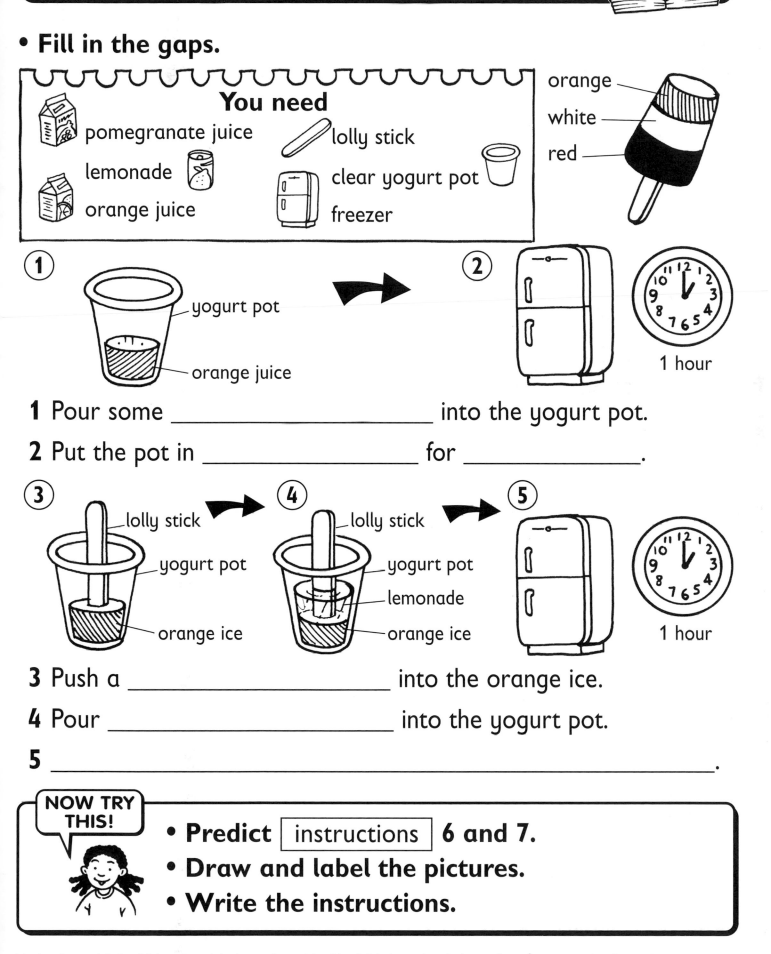

You need

pomegranate juice

lemonade

orange juice

lolly stick

clear yogurt pot

freezer

orange

white

red

① yogurt pot

orange juice

②

1 hour

1 Pour some _____ into the yogurt pot.

2 Put the pot in _____ for _____ .

③ lolly stick

yogurt pot

orange ice

④ lolly stick

yogurt pot

lemonade

orange ice

⑤

1 hour

3 Push a _____ into the orange ice.

4 Pour _____ into the yogurt pot.

5 _____ .

NOW TRY THIS!

- **Predict** | instructions | **6 and 7.**
- **Draw and label the pictures.**
- **Write the instructions.**

Teachers' note Ask the children to read the instructions with a friend. Ask them what the instructions are for and what they need to make the lolly. Point out the 'instruction words' (verbs in the imperative) and remind the children that words like this tell the reader what to do. Compare them with the sentence structure of a recount: 'I poured some orange juice into the yogurt pot.'

100% New Developing Literacy Understanding and Responding to Texts: Ages 6–7
© A & C BLACK

Simon says

- **Look at the pictures.**
- **Write what Simon says.**

Clap your hands.

- **Write three other** [instructions] **for Simon to give.**

Teachers' note You could begin by saying, 'Simon would like you to clap your hands' and then 'I wish you would hop on one leg.' Ask them if this is how to play 'Simon says' and encourage the children to express what Simon says in the conventional way (as instructions). Write up both versions and draw attention to the differences. Point out that in the game the players are given instructions.

100% New Developing Literacy Understanding and Responding to Texts: Ages 6–7
© A & C BLACK

Dragon life cycle

- **Cut out the pictures.**
- **Put them in order.**
- **Glue them onto paper.**
- **Draw arrows to link them.**
- **Tell the** [life cycle] **of a dragon.**

life cycle

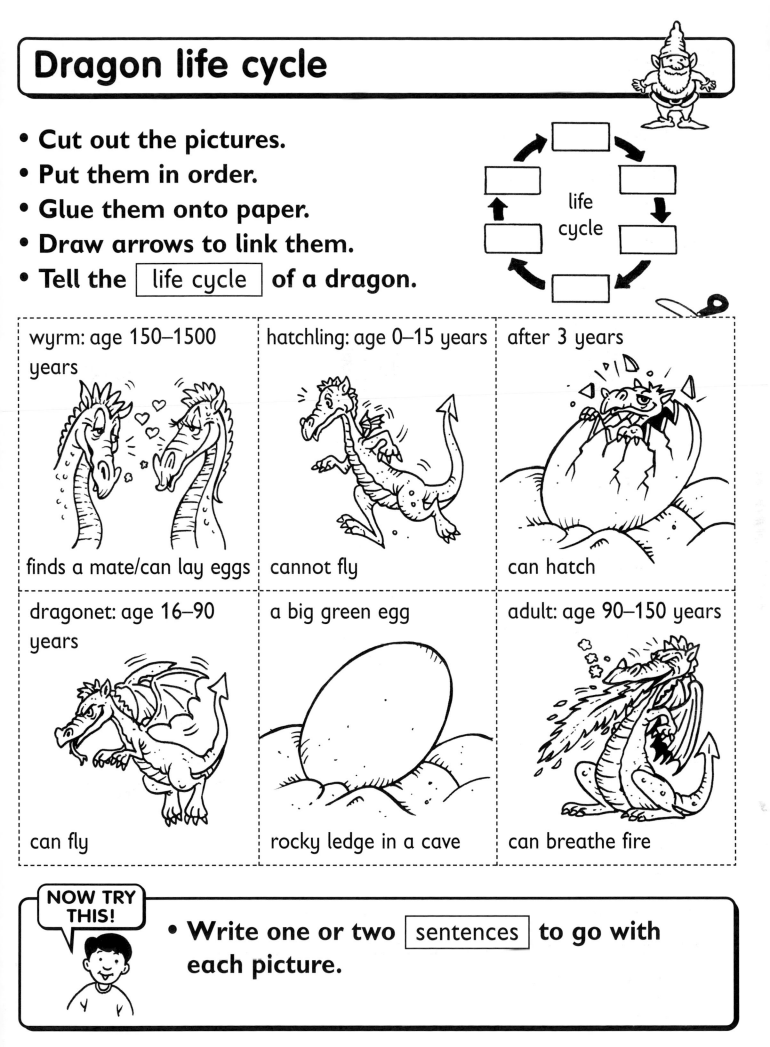

wyrm: age 150–1500 years

finds a mate/can lay eggs

hatchling: age 0–15 years

cannot fly

after 3 years

can hatch

dragonet: age 16–90 years

can fly

a big green egg

rocky ledge in a cave

adult: age 90–150 years

can breathe fire

NOW TRY THIS!

- **Write one or two** [sentences] **to go with each picture.**

Teachers' note Explain that this is non-fiction – an information text, which gives information; it does not tell a story. Ask the children to pick out a picture of the beginning of a dragon's life and to describe it. They can then pick out the next picture and the next and so on, and put them in order. Point out the life cycle diagram and discuss why this is better than a flow-chart in a straight line.

100% New Developing Literacy
Understanding and Responding to Texts: Ages 6–7
© A & C BLACK

Fairyland

• **Fill in the gaps.**

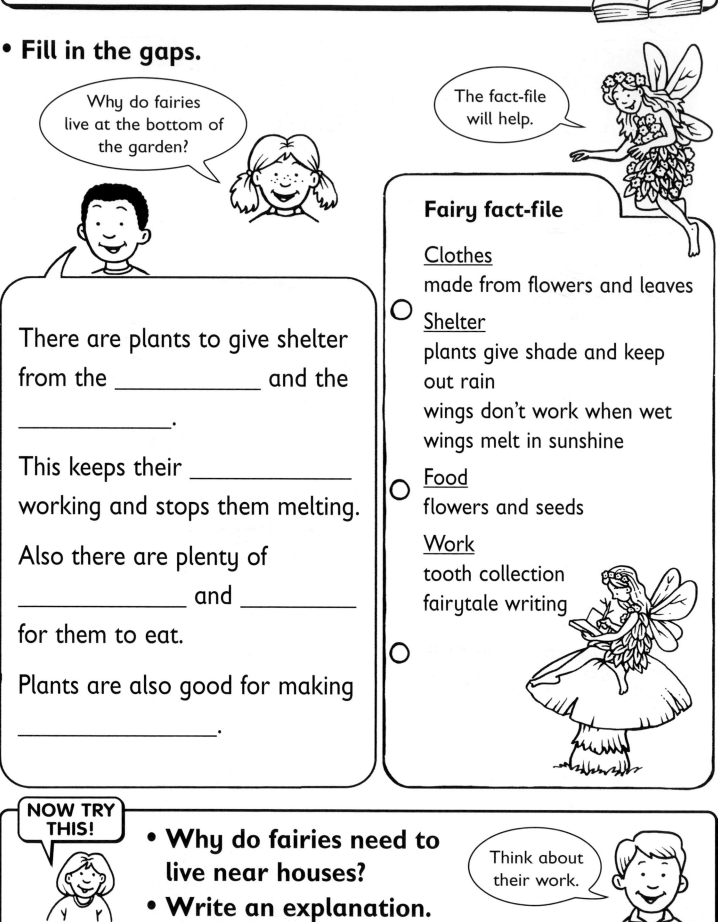

Why do fairies live at the bottom of the garden?

The fact-file will help.

There are plants to give shelter from the _____ and the _____.

This keeps their _____ working and stops them melting.

Also there are plenty of _____ and _____ for them to eat.

Plants are also good for making _____.

Fairy fact-file

Clothes
made from flowers and leaves

○ Shelter
plants give shade and keep out rain
wings don't work when wet
wings melt in sunshine

○ Food
flowers and seeds

Work
tooth collection
fairytale writing

○

NOW TRY THIS!

• **Why do fairies need to live near houses?**
• **Write an explanation.**

Think about their work.

Teachers' note Tell the children that this is a report, not a recount. Use examples to demonstrate the difference. They should use the fact-file to help them to fill the gaps and then use the completed report to help them to answer the question.

100% New Developing Literacy
Understanding and Responding
to Texts: Ages 6–7
© A & C BLACK

Buildings glossary: 1

synagogue	cafe
gurdwara	supermarket
garage	barn
library	house
school	mandir
leisure centre	factory
mosque	church
shop	office

Teachers' note The children could work in groups to help one another to read the words. This should be used with page 38, each page being copied onto paper or card of a different colour. The cards should be cut out. The pages can be used in several ways (see page 38).

100% New Developing Literacy Understanding and Responding to Texts: Ages 6–7
© A & C BLACK

Buildings glossary: 2

A farm building where hay is kept.	A place where people can sit and have a drink and something to eat.
A building where Christians worship.	A building where things are made.
A building where a car is kept.	A building where books are kept.
A building where Sikhs worship.	A building where people live.
A building where you can do sports such as swimming.	A building where Hindus worship.
A building where Muslims worship.	A building where people work at desks.
A building where children go to learn.	A building where you can buy things.
A very big building where you can buy food and other things.	A building where Jews worship.

Teachers' note Use this with page 37. Introduce the term *definition* as in dictionary or glossary definitions. The children could work as a group, matching the definitions to the words or they could place the cards face down and turn over a card from each set to play 'matching pairs', with the winner being the one with the most cards when all have been turned over.

100% New Developing Literacy Understanding and Responding to Texts: Ages 6–7 © A & C BLACK

Miss Muffet's friends

- **Help Little Miss Muffet to find her friends' addresses .**
- **Which way does she need to turn the pages?**
- **Colour the arrow.**

Bo Peep

Humpty Dumpty

L

Lucy Locket
Lost Property Office
Toytown

Georgie Porgie

D

Margery Daw
The Seesaw
Big Field
Toytown

Old King Cole

H

Little Jack Horner
2 Corner Square
Toytown

Polly Flinders

D

Yankee Doodle
8 Donkey Street
Toytown

Jenny Wren

S

Bobby Shaftoe
5 Sea Street
Toytown

Jack Sprat

H

Old Mother Hubbard
Cupboard House
Toytown

NOW TRY THIS!

- **List Little Miss Muffet's friends in alphabetical order .**

Use their last names.

Teachers' note Show the children some address books and ask them how the book is organised to help people to find addresses they have recorded. They should notice that they are in alphabetical order (usually of family name). Remind the children of their work on capital letters for names and ask them first to write the characters' names from the page showing the first letter of their second name.

100% New Developing Literacy
Understanding and Responding
to Texts: Ages 6–7
© A & C BLACK

Fairytale facts

• **Listen to the questions.**

The first to find the answer gets a counter.

The one with most counters wins.

You need

lots of counters

Character	Age	Favourite colour	Pet	Favourite food
Baby Bear	5	Green		
Giant	47	Red		
Gingerbread Man	1	Brown		
Goldilocks	7	Yellow		
Gretel	9	Blue		
Hansel	10	Purple		
Jack	11	Blue		
Red Riding Hood	8	Red		
Troll	92	White		
Witch	33	Pink		

What pet does Jack have?

What colour does Red Riding Hood like best?

How old is Hansel?

What food does Baby Bear like best?

What colour does the Troll like best?

What food does Goldilocks like best?

What pet does the Gingerbread Man have?

How old is the Giant?

What food does the Witch like best?

What pet does Gretel have?

Teachers' note Begin by showing the children the class register and discussing how the names are written in order (in alphabetical order of family name). Note that most of these fairytale characters have only one name and so this register is arranged in alphabetical order of first names. Ensure the children understand that if a character likes something best, then that is his or her favourite.

40

100% New Developing Literacy
Understanding and Responding
to Texts: Ages 6–7
© A & C BLACK

Look it up

- **Read each word on the chart.**
- **Write the first letter.**
- **Find the word in a** ⌐dictionary⌐.
- **Answer the question.**

Word	First letter	Question	Yes or No
newt		Can this grow old?	
quill		Could you write with this?	
ladle		Is this for writing on?	
corgi		Can this talk?	
circuit		Is this a round shape?	
blazer		Could you wear this?	
iguana		Does this eat?	
hearth		Is this a part of your body?	
harp		Is this a drink?	
walrus		Is this an animal?	
square		Does this have six sides?	
budgerigar		Can this fly?	

NOW TRY THIS!

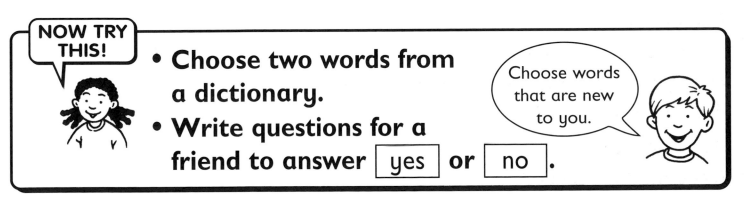

- **Choose two words from a dictionary.**
- **Write questions for a friend to answer** ⌐yes⌐ **or** ⌐no⌐.

Choose words that are new to you.

Teachers' note Show the children how to use a simple picture dictionary. Establish that the words are in alphabetical order to make them easy to find. For a more challenging activity, ask them to cover the chart and to slide the cover down to reveal one word when you say 'Go!' The first to find the word calls out the page number. Invite someone else to read out the definition.

100% New Developing Literacy Understanding and Responding to Texts: Ages 6–7
© A & C BLACK

Book skimmer

- Choose books to help to answer the questions.
- Check title , contents page , sub-headings , index , captions and illustrations .

What is the weather like in Egypt?

How do you make biscuits?

What is it like in a church?

Title of book I chose	Why I chose it	Will it help?

NOW TRY THIS!

- Choose one question and book.
- Make a note of the pages that will help.

Teachers' note Write up a question or read out the first one on this page. Then model how to skim-read an information book to check whether it will help to answer it; draw attention to the contents page, any headings and sub-headings on pages, the index, illustrations and their captions. 'Think aloud' about whether the book contains any useful information.

**100% New Developing Literacy
Understanding and Responding
to Texts: Ages 6–7**
© A & C BLACK

Web skimmer

- Look at two websites about red squirrels.
- What do the websites tell you?

Check the menu , site map and illustrations .

What it tells us about red squirrels

Website title	What they look like	Their size	Where they live	What they eat	What eats them

NOW TRY THIS!

- Write three questions about red squirrels.
- Use the websites to answer them.

Teachers' note Open one of the websites listed on page 6 and look at the home page. Also show the contents page of a book and draw out that they both tell the reader what information they contain and where to find it. Model how to skim-read the home page to check what information it links to and demonstrate how to use the links, the menu and the site map.

Answer finder

- **Colour each number box.**
- **Use the same colour to underline the answer.**

Give each question a different colour.

1	What is a Silky?
2	How can you tell the difference between a Silky and a seal?
3	When do Silkies come onto dry land?
4	How do Silkies change when they come onto land?
5	What do men do when they want to marry a Silky?

Silkies are female sea fairies. They live in the cold seas around northern Scotland.

They look like seals except that Silkies have very bright eyes.

During nights when there is a full moon Silkies often come onto the land to dance in the moonlight. They shed their sealskin and change their shape to look human. When a Silky is in human shape she has webbed fingers and toes, like a duck. She can swim under water for a long time.

She hides her sealskin in a safe place. She has to put it on again in order to go back to sea. There are many tales from Scotland of men stealing a Silky's skin so that he can keep her on dry land and marry her. Silkies are said to make very good wives, but they always long for the sea. If they find their skins they go back to their seal shape and disappear into the sea. Anyone who damages a Silky sealskin will have bad luck for ever.

NOW TRY THIS!

- **Write** notes **to answer the questions.**

Do not write sentences.

Teachers' note Read the first question with the children and model how to find the answer by reading the text. Point out the words *Silkies are*. Think aloud: 'Let's see what it says Silkies are – "Silkies are female sea fairies" – that means a silky is a female sea fairy.' Underline the text which gave the answer. Ask the children to do the same for the other questions.

100% New Developing Literacy Understanding and Responding to Texts: Ages 6–7 © A & C BLACK

Seashore scanner

- **Find a book about the seashore.**
- **Use it to help you to fill the gaps.**

Work with a friend.

A seashore can be covered with _____, shingle, pebbles, mud or rocks. Some plants can grow in these salty places. Two of them are _____ and marram grass.

On most beaches you can find shells. Shells are the _____ of sea creatures. Their skeleton is outside their body. Two sea creatures that have shells are the _____ and the _____.

An animal that has no shell of its own is the _____ crab. It finds a shell from a _____ animal instead and, when it grows too big for the shell it finds a _____ one.

Rock pools are the homes of many sea creatures, such as _____. Crabs have a hard shell, a pair of pincers and _____ legs.

Some birds nest near the sea. The _____ and the _____ nest on cliffs.

NOW TRY THIS!

- **Write two questions about the seashore.**
- **Use books to find answers.**
- **Write the answers.**

Teachers' note Ask the children if this is an information or fiction text. Help them to point out the clues: for example, it describes the seashore and gives facts; it does not tell a story. Provide information books about the seashore and remind the children how to skim them to locate information and then to scan the text to find the exact information they want.

100% New Developing Literacy Understanding and Responding to Texts: Ages 6–7 © A & C BLACK

Island reports

- **Find out about an island.**

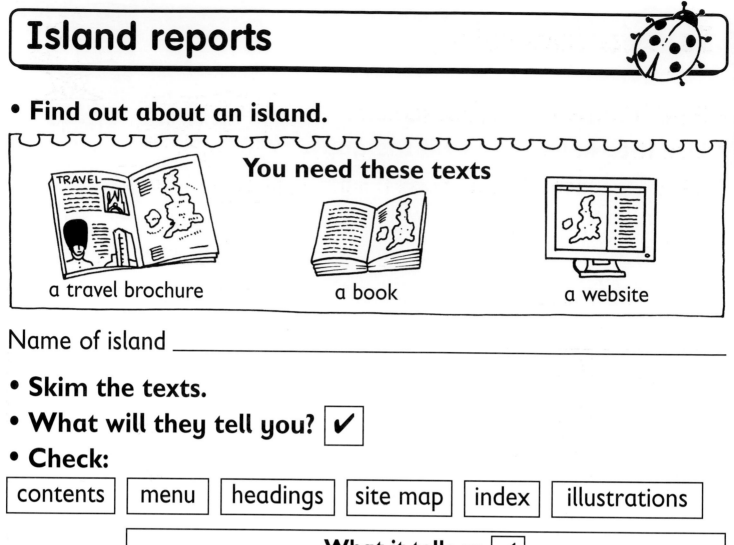

You need these texts

a travel brochure   a book   a website

Name of island _____

- **Skim the texts.**
- **What will they tell you?** ✔
- **Check:**

| contents | menu | headings | site map | index | illustrations |

Text	What it tells us ✔					
	Where the island is	Which sea it is in	How big it is	What the land is like	What people have built	What work they do there
Travel brochure						
Book						
Website						

NOW TRY THIS!

- **Write three questions about the island.**
- **Make sure you know the answers!**

Teachers' note This page could be linked with work in geography on an island home. Remind the children that they do not need to read the leaflet and book from cover to cover and that they need not read every word on the website (see *Notes on the activities*, pages 6 and 10). Also remind them how to scan these information texts in order to find the information they want.

100% New Developing Literacy Understanding and Responding to Texts: Ages 6–7
© A & C BLACK

Island fact-file

- **Find out about an island.**
- **Use the Internet.**
- **Check:** | menu | site map | links | photos | maps |
- **Record what you found out.**

	Island	
Size	**Where it is**	
<u>Landscape</u> ✔		
moorland ☐	hills ☐	forests ☐
farmland ☐	lakes ☐	rivers ☐
<u>Coast</u> ✔		
beaches ☐	cliffs ☐	bays ☐
sand dunes ☐	rocks ☐	marshes ☐
<u>Buildings</u> ✔		
houses ☐	shops ☐	factories ☐
churches ☐	other places of worship ☐	
post offices ☐	banks ☐	garages ☐

NOW TRY THIS!

- **Write a question about a building on the island.**
- **Give it to a friend to find the answer.**

Teachers' note This follows on from page 46. Once the children have located the type of information they want, encourage them to find out about a specific aspect of the island – the land and what has been built on it. Once they have recorded the facts you could also ask them to construct sentences about the natural and built features of the island.

100% New Developing Literacy
Understanding and Responding
to Texts: Ages 6–7
© A & C BLACK

Key words map

- **What do visitors need to know about this island?**
- **Write** key words **.**

places to sleep

Come and stay on our beautiful island!

SHOP BANK GARAGE

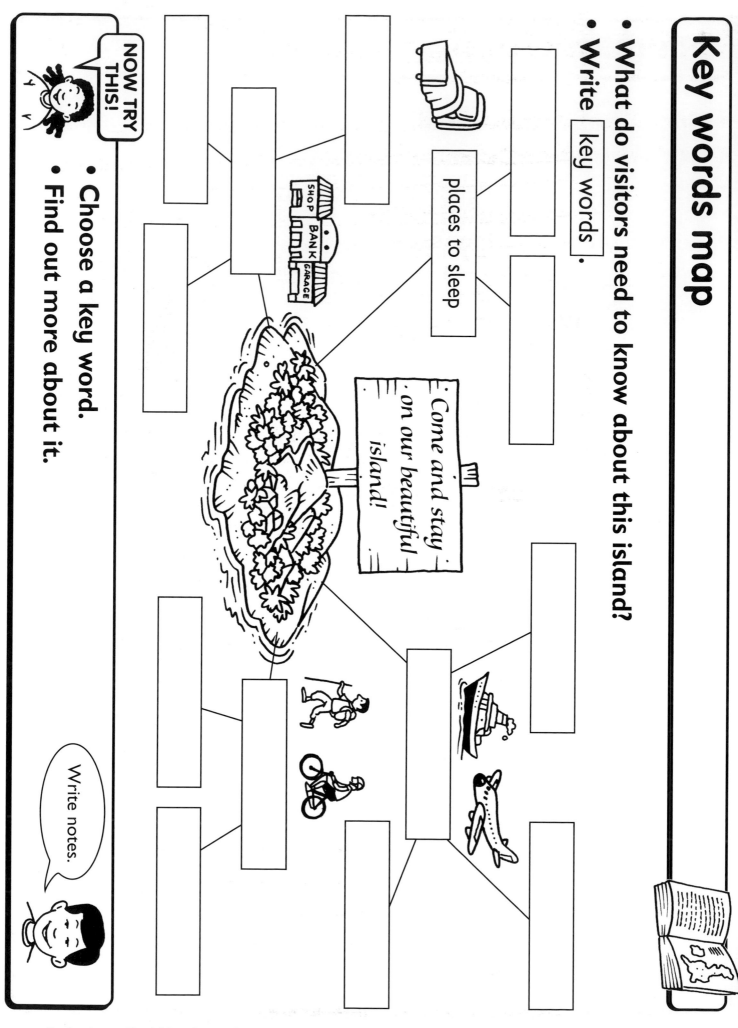

NOW TRY THIS!

- **Choose a key word.**
- **Find out more about it.**

Write notes.

Teachers' note The children first need to have scanned information texts about an island, in connection with work in geography lessons. Read the question and ask the children to brainstorm the types of things visitors need to know (one has been supplied for them). They can scan the texts again to find names of hotels and B&Bs, transport and so on.

100% New Developing Literacy
Understanding and Responding
to Texts: Ages 6–7
© A & C BLACK

Guy Fawkes information race: 1

This race is for two teams.

- **Find the answers as quickly as you can.**

Team 1 uses books.

Team 2 uses the Internet.

- **Tick the answers ✔.**

Team: 1 ☐   Using: books ☐

2 ☐   Internet ☐

Questions	Answers	
Where was Guy Fawkes born?	☐ London ☐ Paris	☐ York
What was his religion?	☐ Roman Catholic ☐ Anglican	☐ Sikh
How long ago did he live?	☐ 10 years ☐ 400 years	☐ 100 years
Which king did he try to kill?	☐ James I ☐ William the Conqueror	☐ Henry VIII
How did he die?	☐ Illness ☐ Electric chair	☐ Hanging

NOW TRY THIS!

- **Which team won?**
- **Discuss why.**

Teachers' note The children need access to a book and a website about Guy Fawkes (see *Notes on the activities*, page 10). Teams are probably best fairly small. You could copy this page onto an interactive whiteboard, cover the questions and reveal one at a time. The challenge is to be the first team to find the answer. Encourage the others to check if the answer given is correct.

100% New Developing Literacy
Understanding and Responding
to Texts: Ages 6–7
© A & C BLACK

49

Guy Fawkes information race: 2

- **Think about a book and a website.**
- **What did you like?**
- **What did you not like?**

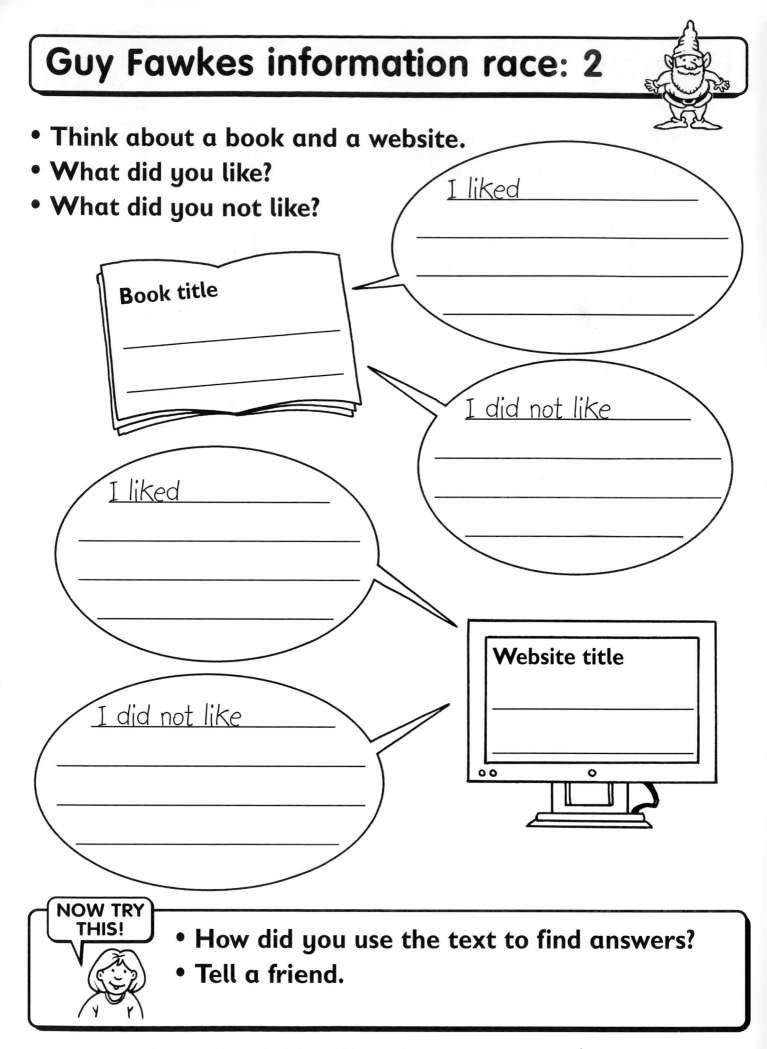

I liked _____
_____
_____
_____

Book title
_____
_____

I did not like _____
_____
_____
_____

I liked _____
_____
_____
_____

Website title
_____
_____

I did not like _____
_____
_____
_____

NOW TRY THIS!

- **How did you use the text to find answers?**
- **Tell a friend.**

Teachers' note This page could be used to help the children to judge the texts they used for page 49 or for a comparison of books and websites on any other topic. Point out where to record the title of the text. What was good and what was bad about it? They could consider the contents page/home page and menu, index, site map, illustrations, how easy the text was to read and so on.

100% New Developing Literacy
Understanding and Responding
to Texts: Ages 6–7
© A & C BLACK

Note it

Meera has made notes about materials she saw in the street.

Meera

Use my notes to write sentences.

Key

b   bendy

h   hard

s   strong

t   tough

tr   transparent

Material	Used for	Why
stone	kerb	t
wood	door	h
plastic	bags	b
metal	grid	s
glass	window	tr

Glass is used for windows because it is _____.

This material is strong: _____.

Stone is used for kerbs because it is _____.

Wood is used for doors because it is _____.

Plastic is used for bags because it is _____.

Teachers' note Explain that making notes means recording information in a quick way and that one way of doing this is to use a chart with headings. Tell the children that once they have made a note of all the information they need they can then write about it in sentences.

100% New Developing Literacy
Understanding and Responding
to Texts: Ages 6–7
© A & C BLACK

51

Sea song

- **Read the poem aloud.**
- **Say the missing words.**
- **Write the missing words.**

Sea song

Sea-shell, sea-shell,
Murmuring sand,
Murmuring sand.

Sea-shell, sea-shell,
Far-away land,

_____ .

_____ ,

Sing in my hand,

_____ .

_____ ,

I'll understand,
You'll _____ .

James Kirkup

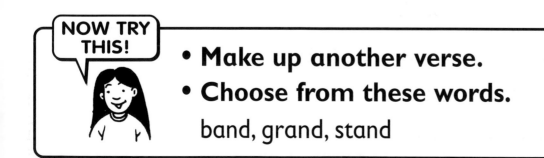

NOW TRY THIS!

- **Make up another verse.**
- **Choose from these words.**

  band, grand, stand

Teachers' note Read the first verse of the poem aloud, then begin the second verse; stop after *land*. If the children cannot continue, point out the pattern of the first verse (the second line is repeated). Reread the second verse and let the children complete the missing part orally. Ask them to talk to a friend about the missing lines in the third verse. Point out that the fourth verse is slightly different.

100% New Developing Literacy Understanding and Responding to Texts: Ages 6–7
© A & C BLACK

Anna Elise

- **Follow the route as you read the poem.**

Anna Elise

Anna Elise jumped with surprise;
The surprise was so quick, it played her a trick.

The trick was so rare, she jumped on a chair;
The chair was so frail, she jumped in a pail.

The pail was so wet, she jumped in a net;
The net was so small, she jumped on a ball;

The ball was so round, she jumped on the ground;
And ever since then she's been turning around.

Anonymous

NOW TRY THIS!

- **Change the words of the poem.**
- **Use these words.**

Billy Block, shock

Teachers' note You could copy the poem onto an interactive whiteboard or make paper copies for each child. Read it aloud with the children and show them how to follow the circular route with a finger. Discuss why it is circular (Anna Elise ends up turning around and around).

100% New Developing Literacy Understanding and Responding to Texts: Ages 6–7 © A & C BLACK

Fire! Fire!

- ## Read 'Fire! Fire!'
- ## Make up another poem like this.

Fire! Fire!

"Fire! Fire!" says Obadiah.

"Where? Where?" says Mrs Pear.

"Behind the rocks," says Doctor Fox.

"Put it out!" says Mr Trout.

"I've no bucket," says Lord MacTuckett.

"Use my shoe," says Miss Agatha Drewe.

Anonymous

The speech bubbles will help.

"Stop thief!"

Miss McCrieff

Where? Where?

Mr O'Hare

At the bank.

Mrs Crank

Phone the police.

My phone won't work.

I'll use mine.

NOW TRY THIS!

- ## • Check your poem for rhyme.
- ## • Change any words that do not rhyme.

_____

_____

_____

_____

_____

_____

_____

_____

_____

Teachers' note Invite the children to read the poem in unison, then ask them which words rhyme. Discuss what they notice about the positions of these rhyming words (they are within the same line). This is an example of internal rhyme but this term is not yet introduced to the children. Ask them to make up names to rhyme with the last word of the last three speech bubbles.

100% New Developing Literacy Understanding and Responding to Texts: Ages 6–7
© A & C BLACK

Bouncing

- **Read the poem in two groups.**

One group reads the main words.	**The other group reads** *bounce* **and** *bouncing*.

- **Jump up and down as if bouncing on a bed.**
- **Stand or sit still.**

Bouncing

My mum,
bounce,
doesn't like it.
My dad,
bounce,
goes out of his head.
But I love to *bounce,*
bounce, bounce
on top of my bed.

My mum,
bounce,
calls out.
My dad,
bounce,
shouts from the hall.
But when I'm *bouncing,*
bouncing, bouncing,
I take no
bounce
notice at all.

Simon James

NOW TRY THIS!

- **Make up your own words for the poem.**

Keep the bounce and bouncing.

Teachers' note The children need plenty of space for this poem as one group is going to bounce up and down energetically throughout (ask them to bounce as if they are bouncing on a bed) and read the main words in a breathless way, with another group saying *bounce* in the appropriate places.

100% New Developing Literacy Understanding and Responding to Texts: Ages 6–7
© A & C BLACK

Shape match

• **Copy the poems onto the shapes.**

Buzzing busily
bustling around the begonias.

Change the size
of the writing.
Use colours.

Fly flitting fast
fussing and feeding.

Whiskers twitching
Long back arching
Poised to pounce.

Wriggling, writhing
slipping, sliding.

NOW TRY THIS!

• **Draw a shape for this poem.**

Eight long legs waiting in a web.

• **Write the poem in the shape.**

Teachers' note Copy this page onto A3 paper to give the children room to write in the shapes. Ask them to read the words in the boxes and to decide which animal they describe. They can then choose the appropriate shape to write them on. This could be used to introduce shape poems or to summarise what they have learned about them.

100% New Developing Literacy Understanding and Responding to Texts: Ages 6–7
© A & C BLACK

56

Quiet poems: 1

- **Listen to the poem.**
- **What can you hear if you lie in bed very still and very quiet?**
- **Talk to a friend about these sounds.**
- **Write them on the notepad.**

Work with a friend.

Night Sounds

When I lie in bed
I think I can hear
The stars being switched on
I think I can.

And I think I can hear
The moon
Breathing.

But I have to be still.
So still.
All the house is sleeping.
Except for me.

Then I think I can hear it.

Berlie Doherty

Notepad

the birds snoring

NOW TRY THIS!

- **Complete the verse with your own words.**

When I lie in bed
I think I can hear

_____

_____

Teachers' note Have the children sitting very still and quiet and, if possible, darken the room slightly. If you have time you could pin up a few stars and a moon before you begin. Read the poem softly and discuss it in hushed voices: ask the children what quiet things they think they can hear at night. You might need to suggest some: for example, the sky turning over, an owl blinking.

100% New Developing Literacy
Understanding and Responding
to Texts: Ages 6–7
© A & C BLACK

Quiet poems: 2

- **Read the poem to yourself.**
- **How will you read it aloud?**
- **What actions will you do?**
- **Write notes in the boxes.**

Shhhhhhhh!

How to read

in a whisper

_____

_____

_____

_____

_____

_____

_____

_____

_____

_____

_____

Listen

Shhhhhhhh!

Sit still, very still

And listen.

Listen to wings

Lighter than eyelashes

Stroking the air.

Know what the thin breeze

Whispers on high

To the coconut trees.

Listen and hear.

Telcine Turner

Actions

put my finger to
my lips

_____

_____

_____

_____

_____

_____

_____

_____

_____

_____

NOW TRY THIS!

- **Write six words that sound quiet.**
- **Use some of these to help you to write a line for a quiet poem.**

Teachers' note The children should first have read some quiet poems or completed page 57. Ask them to read it to themselves and to think about how they will read it aloud, then ask them to read it in unison (this could be carried out in small groups at different times). Ask them which parts told them it should be read quietly. They could underline these.

100% New Developing Literacy Understanding and Responding to Texts: Ages 6–7
© A & C BLACK

Words and pictures

- **Match the words to the pictures.**
- **Write them on the lines.**

---

dee dum, dee dum

dum, dum, dum

---

tip-toe, tip-toe

stop – listen

Whoosh! Whizz!

Stars scream

Chattering wheels

Rushing along

_____

_____

_____

_____

NOW TRY THIS!

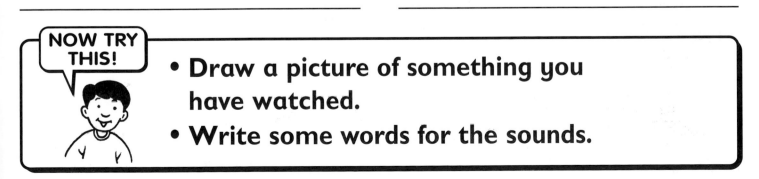

- **Draw a picture of something you have watched.**
- **Write some words for the sounds.**

Teachers' note Before giving out copies of this sheet, invite four volunteers to read the four sets of words aloud to the class. Ask the other children if that is how they would read them. Remind them of rhymes/songs that use these effects: for example, *I hear thunder...*; *Horsey horsey, don't you stop...* Ask them what pictures they see in their minds when they hear the words.

100% New Developing Literacy Understanding and Responding to Texts: Ages 6–7 © A & C BLACK

Rough or smooth

- **Read the words aloud.**
- **Listen to the** sounds **.**
- **Write them in the shapes.**

Do the words sound rough or smooth?

cool	gravel	pillow	rocky
cracker	harsh	prickle	roll
fleece	jagged	puff	snatch
flower	lullaby	rattle	velvet

rough

smooth

NOW TRY THIS!

- **Write two more** rough **words.**
- **Write two more** smooth **words.**

Teachers' note Explain that you are going to say a word and that the children should decide if it sounds rough or smooth. (Say *rough* in a rough way and *smooth* in a smooth way.) It doesn't matter whether or not they know the words. Say a few more words for extra practice: *gruff, melody, scratchy, scrape, seamless.* Why is there sometimes a connection between the sound of a word and its meaning?

60

100% New Developing Literacy
Understanding and Responding
to Texts: Ages 6–7
© A & C BLACK

Wild words

• **Finish the pairs of words.**

> The first sounds must be the same.

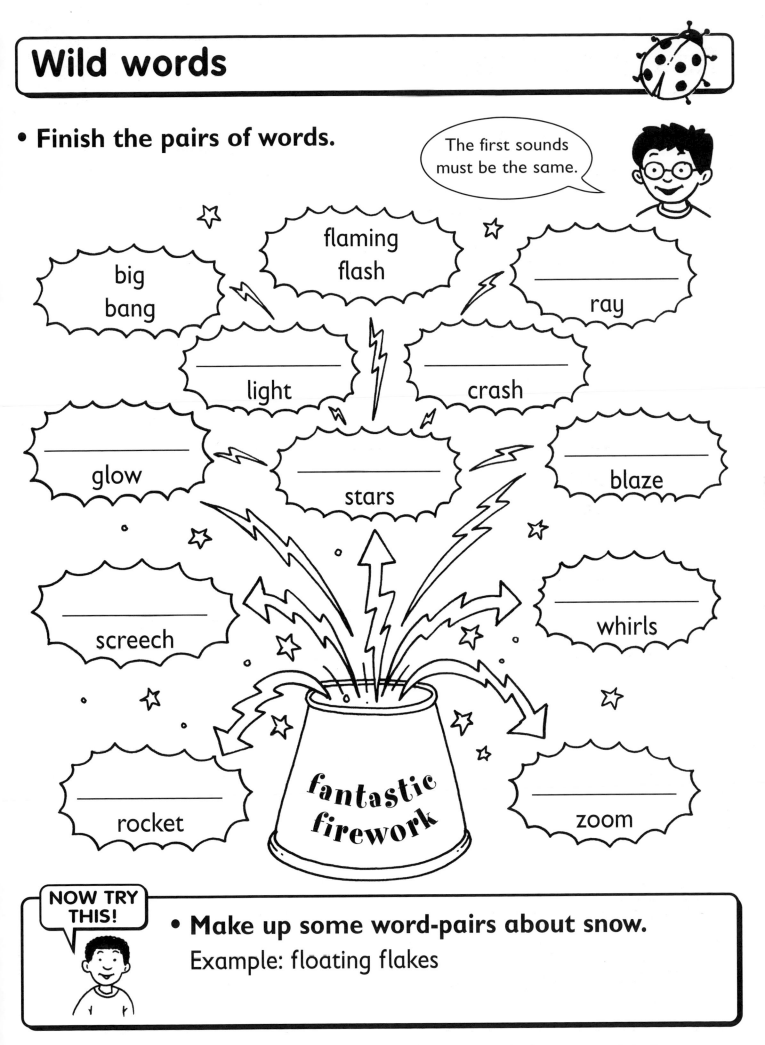

flaming flash

big bang

_____ ray

_____ light

_____ crash

_____ glow

_____ stars

blaze

_____ screech

_____ whirls

_____ rocket

fantastic firework

_____ zoom

NOW TRY THIS!

• **Make up some word-pairs about snow.**

Example: floating flakes

Teachers' note Say a few alliterative phrases and ask the children what they notice about the sounds: for example, *fuzzy felt, flip-flops, zig-zag.* Read some poems containing alliteration and point out how this can create an effect such as silence, a rough sea and so on. Encourage the children to think of words which help to create an effect, such as *whizzing whirls, crunching crash, gleaming glow.*

100% New Developing Literacy Understanding and Responding to Texts: Ages 6–7 © A & C BLACK

A funny little man

- **Think of words to write in the gaps.**
- **Write the words.**
- **Read the poem with a friend.**

Dan, Dan, the funny little man,
Washed his face in the frying pan,
Combed his hair with the leg of the chair,
Dan, Dan, the funny little man.

Dan, Dan, the funny little man,
Brushed his teeth with a _____,
Blew his nose with _____,
Dan, Dan, the funny little man.

Dan, Dan, the funny little man,
Cleaned his shoes with a _____,
Washed his shirt in _____,
Dan, Dan, the funny little man.

Dan, Dan, the funny little man,
Washed his car with a _____,
Shaved his face with _____,
Dan, Dan, the funny little man.

NOW TRY THIS!

- **Make up a verse for a poem about a silly teacher.**

Teachers' note Allow the children time to read the poem with a friend and have fun trying out different words in the gaps: for example, *brushed his teeth with a leg of lamb, blew his nose with the garden hose, cleaned his shoes with a slice of ham, washed his shirt in a bowl of dirt, washed his car with a bucket of bran, shaved his face with a piece of plaice.*

100% New Developing Literacy
Understanding and Responding
to Texts: Ages 6–7
© A & C BLACK

Mrs Brown went to town

- **Sing the first verse about Mrs Brown.**
- **Write three new verses.**
- **Sing your poem.**

Mrs Brown went to town,
Riding on a pony,
When she came back she lost her hat,
And called on Miss Maloney.

Mrs Brown went to town,
Riding on a push-bike,
When she came back she lost her hat,
And called on _____.

Mrs Brown went to town,
Riding on a tandem,
When she came back she lost her hat,
And called on _____.

Mrs Brown went to town,
Driving a Mercedes,
When she came back she lost her hat,
And called on _____.

NOW TRY THIS!

- **Make up a verse about a man who went to war.**

Teachers' note Sing the first verse with the children to the tune of *Yankee Doodle*, then let them sing the rest with their friends, making up the missing parts. Stop them at intervals and invite volunteers to sing a verse to the class. They can then choose the versions they want to write. You could write this or key it as a display to which the children could add new verses (perhaps on a 'graffiti wall').

100% New Developing Literacy Understanding and Responding to Texts: Ages 6–7 © A & C BLACK

Tongue-twister match-up

Beginnings	Endings
Lesley licked a yellow lolly;	the fritters Fred fried were fine.
Fred fried four fritters;	the dishes Dizzy Dora dropped were dusty.
William wore red wellies;	the lolly Lesley licked was yellow.
Terry tried to taste the treacle;	in Shelly's silly shoe shop.
Shelly sold silly shoes;	and William waded in the river.
Dizzy Dora dropped the dishes;	the treacle trickled down Terry's trousers.
Gordon Green grows ghosts in his garden;	the best bananas are bent by Ben.
Ben Bone bends bananas;	Gordon grins as the ghosts grow.

Teachers' note Cut out the beginnings and the endings or ask the children to do so and they can then match up each beginning with an ending. Or give each child a beginning or an ending and ask them to read them aloud and find their partners.

100% New Developing Literacy Understanding and Responding to Texts: Ages 6–7
© A & C BLACK